A Book *of* Marionettes

by
Helen Haiman Joseph

Copyright © 2013 Read Books Ltd.
This book is copyright and may not be
reproduced or copied in any way without
the express permission of the publisher in writing

British Library Cataloguing-in-Publication Data
A catalogue record for this book is available from the
British Library

Introduction to
Puppets and Marionettes

A puppet is an inanimate object or representational figure, animated or manipulated by a puppeteer. They are used in 'puppetry'; a very ancient form of theatre. There are a staggering variety of puppets, and they can be made of a wide range of materials, dependent on their form and intended use.

Puppetry was first practised in Ancient Greece and the oldest written records of puppetry can be found in the works of Herodotus and Xenophon, dating from the fifth century BC. The Greek word translated as 'puppet' is 'νευρόσπαστος' (*nevrospastos*), which literally means 'drawn by strings, string-pulling', from 'νε?ρον' (*nevron*), meaning either 'sinew or string' and 'σπάω' (*spa?*), meaning 'draw or pull.' Aristotle (384–322 BC) discussed puppets in his work *On the Motion of Animals*. He stated that the movements of animals may be compared with those of automatic puppets, 'which are set going on the occasion of a tiny movement; the levers are released, and strike the twisted strings against one another.'

Puppetry by its nature is a flexible and inventive medium, and many puppet companies work with combinations of puppet forms, and incorporate real objects into their performances. They might, for example, incorporate 'performing objects' such as torn paper for snow, or a sign board with words as narrative devices within a production. Some key types of puppet are 'the black light puppet'; a form puppetry where the mannequins are operated on a stage, lit only with ultraviolet lighting. 'The hand puppet' (better known as the glove puppet) is controlled by one hand which occupies the interior of the puppet. The Punch and Judy puppets are familiar examples of this type. Larger varieties of hand puppets place the puppeteer's hand in just the puppet's head, and the body then hangs over the entire arm. Perhaps one of the most interesting, and ethereal types of puppet is the 'shadow puppet'; a cut-out figure, held between a source of light and a translucent screen. Shadow puppets can form solid silhouettes or be decorated with various amounts of cut-out details, even with coloured light introduced to provide yet another dimension. Javanese shadow puppets known as 'Wayang Kulit' are a classic example of this.

'Marionettes' are one of the oldest forms of performance puppetry, the term meaning 'little Mary' in French. Both Archimedes and Plato's work refers directly to Marionettes, and the Iliad and the Odyssey were first presented using these mannequins. Our present day puppetry probably extends back to these plays, performed to the 'common people' of the fifth century BC. Marionettes, or 'string puppets', are suspended and controlled by a number of strings, plus sometimes a central rod attached to a control bar held from above by the puppeteer. Basic strings for operation are usually attached to the head, back, hands (to control the arms) and just above the knee (to control the legs). This form of puppetry is complex and sophisticated to operate, requiring greater manipulative control than a finger, glove or rod puppet. In modern times, marionettes are sometimes referred to as 'puppets', but the term 'marionettes' is more precise, distinguishing them from other forms of puppetry, such as finger, glove, rod and shadow puppetry.

In the eighteenth century, operas were specifically composed for marionettes, Gluck, Haydn, de Falla and Respighi all composed adult operas for marionettes. Today in Salzburg in Austria, the Salzburg Marionette Theatre still continues the tradition of presenting full length opera using marionettes in their own purpose built theatre. In the UK, the renaissance of Marionettes during the late nineteenth and early twentieth century was driven by W. H. Whanslaw and Waldo Lanchester, two of the co-founders of the *British Puppet and Model Theatre Guild*. The only purpose-built UK marionette theatre, founded by Eric Bramall and continued by Chris Somerville, is *The Harlequin Puppet Theatre* (built 1958) in Rhos on Sea, North Wales. There are many other theatres across the country however, that occasionally perform with marionettes. With the rise of television and film, marionettes found a rise in popularity especially in children's programming. The Disney produced story of Pinocchio was released in 1940 is solely focused on the adventures of a marionette. In the following decade, Bil Baird and Cora Eisenberg presented a great number of marionette shows for television, and were also responsible for the Lonely Goatherd sequence from the classic film *The Sound of Music*.

From the 1950s onwards, the BBC in the United Kingdom produced a wide series of marionette programmes for children, most notably from The *BBC Television Puppet Theatre* based in *Lime Grove Studios* from 1955–1964. Usually under the title *Watch With Mother*, the various programmes included *Whirligig*, *The Woodentops*, *Bill and Ben*, *Muffin The Mule* and *Andy Pandy*. Later in the 1960s, Gerry Anderson with his wife, Sylvia Anderson made a number of hit series, *Fireball XL5*, *Stingray* and *Thunderbirds*, which pioneered a technique combining marionettes and electronics. This allowed for radio control moving of the mouth of a marionette, and became known as 'supermarionation.' As is clear from this incredibly brief history, the purpose, nature and capabilities of puppets and especially marionettes has changed enormously over the centuries. They still continue to delight and fascinate many audiences though, young and old alike.

To my Father
ELIAS HAIMAN
*With pride and love for the brave simplicity
and gentle nobility of his life*

Note

THE story of the marionette is endless, in fact it has neither beginning nor end. The marionette has been everywhere and is everywhere. One cannot write of the puppets without saying more than one had intended and less than one desired: there is such a piquant insistency in them. The purpose of this book is altogether modest, but the length of it has grown to be presumptuous. As to its merit, that must be found in the subject matter and in the sources from which the material was gathered. If this volume is but a sign-post pointing the way to better historians and friends of the puppets and through them on to more puppet play it will have proven merit enough.

The bibliography appended is a far from complete list of puppet literature. It includes, however, the most important works of modern times upon marionettes and much comment, besides, that is casual or curious or close at hand.

The author is under obligation to those friendly individuals who generously gave of their time and

NOTE

interest and whose suggestions, explanations and kind assistance have made possible this publication. There are many who have been gracious and helpful, among them particularly Mrs. Maurice Browne, Mr. Michael Carmichael Carr, Professor A. K. Coomaraswamy, Mr. Stewart Culin, Dr. Jesse Walter Fewkes, Mr. Henry Festing Jones, Dr. Berthold Laufer, Mr. Richard Laukhuff, Mr. J. Arthur MacLean, Professor Brander Matthews, Dr. Ida Trent O'Neil, Mr. Raymond O'Neil, Mr. Alfred Powell, Dr. R. Meyer Riefstahl, Mr. Tony Sarg, and Mr. G. Bernard Shaw.

Above all, however, acknowledgment is due to the steady encouragement and interested criticism of Ernest Joseph. Although he did not live to see the finished volume, his stimulating buoyancy and excellent judgment constantly inspired the composition of this simple account of puppets.

Contents

How I Came to Write a Book on Puppets, 9
Puppets of Antiquity, 14
Oriental Puppets, 24
Puppets of Italy and Southern Europe, 50
The Puppets in France, 81
Puppet Shows of Germany and of other Continental Countries, 113
Puppetry in England, 143
The Marionettes in America, 164
Toy Theatres and Puppet Plays for Children, 192
A Plea for Polichinelle, 203
Behind the Scenes, 216
Construction of a Marionette Stage, 225
Bibliography, 229
Index, 233

Illustrations

SHADOW FIGURES DISCOVERED IN EGYPT BY DR. PAUL KAHLE	End-papers
DRYAD AND TWO FAUNS	Frontispiece
JOINTED DOLLS OR PUPPETS	18
SIAMESE SHADOWS	22
JAVANESE WAYANG FIGURES	24
JAVANESE ROUNDED MARIONETTES	26
WAYANG FIGURES FROM THE ISLAND OF BALI	28
BURMESE PUPPETS	30
CINGALESE PUPPETS	32
EAST INDIAN PUPPETS	34
TURKISH SHADOW FIGURE OF KARAGHUEZ	36
CHINESE PUPPETS	38
CHINESE SHADOW-PLAY FIGURES	40
CHINESE SHADOW-PLAY FIGURES	42
OLD JAPANESE PUPPET HEADS	44
JAPANESE PRINT	48
A WOODEN ITALIAN PUPPET	52
MEDIÆVAL MARIONETTES	54
ITALIAN FIGURES USED FOR CHRISTMAS CRIB	56
PULCINELLA IN ITALY	58
ITALIAN PUPPET BALLET	62
WOODEN SPANISH PUPPETS	78
GEORGE SAND'S PUPPET THEATRE AT NOHANT	92
PUPPETS OF GEORGE SAND'S THEATRE AT NOHANT	94
PUPPETS OF LEMERCIER DE NEUVILLE	96
TABLEAU (CHAT NOIR)	98

ILLUSTRATIONS

Guignol and Gnafron	110
Marionette Theatre of Munich Artists	130
Marionettes of Richard Teschner, Vienna	134
Bohemian Puppets	136
Punch Hangs the Hangman	148
Old English Puppets	156
Gair Wilkinson and Assistant at Work on the Bridge of their Puppet Theatre	158
Marionettes Employed in Ceremonial Drama of the American Indians	166
Italian Marionette Show	172
Marionettes at the Chicago Little Theatre	174
The Death of Chopin	178
Shadowy Waters	182
Tony Sarg's Marionettes behind the Scenes	184
A Trick Puppet	188
German Puppet Show for Children	196
English Toy Theatre	200
Patterns for the Marionette Body Drawn by Max Kalish	222
Diagrams for the Construction of a Marionette Stage	226

How I Came to Write a Book on Puppets

WE were rehearsing laboriously. Some of our marionettes were finished; the rest we borrowed from the cast of *Tintagiles*. The effect was curious with Belangere and Ygraine acting as sentinels in their blue and green gowns.

The play we were rehearsing was eventually given up. For various reasons the little puppets about to be presented to you never displayed themselves before the public. Undeniable facts, but for my story quite irrelevant and inconsequential.

It was late and everyone else in the house had retired. I sat up all alone, diligently sewing. Alone? Grouped around me in various stages of completion sat the miniature members of the cast. I worked quietly, much absorbed. Off in the corner there was a clock, ticking.

The Chief Prophet of the Stars lay in my hands, impressive by virtue of his flowing white beard, even without the high purple hat. I rested a moment, straightening a weary back. One long white arm of his was pointing at me. He said: "Do not pity yourself. Despite your backache you are having a lovely time." I am sure he said this. I did not answer. How could I? It was true. Near by was the black-

MARIONETTES

robed Priest with the auburn beard. "Even so," he agreed, "her fingers are happy: her tongue may not complain!"

"It is an honor to be permitted to dress us," pompously proclaimed the Chamberlain. He was perched upon the mantel. His queer, stiff beard having been but recently shellacked was now in the process of drying. He was a balloon shaped, striking fellow arrayed in orange.

"She must finish my high hat tonight," said the Chief Prophet of the Stars, "and see that my whiskers are decently trimmed. Then she may retire."

"No," whimpered one of the spotty Spies from the floor, "she promised to brighten my spots for tomorrow." Then, in a loud aside, "She will probably get my strings twisted while painting the spots. Serve her right. She was too impatient to show me off yesterday. One should finish the *spots first*, say I." Ungrateful wretch, to be grumbling! But he crawled and crept along the stage so wonderfully I hadn't the heart to chide him.

I sat the Chief Prophet upon my knee, crossly. His long arm protested stiffly. I pulled the high hat down over his ominous brows. "It isn't right," he said. It wasn't. I took it off. How trying it must be for him to have so clumsy a handmaiden. "Don't pin it!" he commanded. "Rip it and sew it neatly." I picked up the scissors and ripped. Then I sewed on in silence.

The marionettes, however, had many things to say.

"She is not as thorough as might be desired," stated the Chamberlain. "Indeed, I fear that in the manipulating also she is only an amateur with no profound knowledge of the craft. Here am I, still dissatisfied with the bow I make to His Majesty. I know just how I should bow. Who would question my knowledge of etiquette? I shall not be content with anything but *the correct* bow, dignified and, in its way, imposing as the nod of a King. It must be just so and not otherwise but *how will she do it?* She has tried front strings and back strings and innumerable petty expedients. She calls herself a puppeteer: let her devise a way and that shortly! I scorn to display vexation but it perturbs me not a little as the moment approaches for me to bow and the bow, ahem . . . refuses to function fittingly."

"Try on the hat and do not be diverted by such details!" commands the Chief Prophet. I sit him up seriously. "It will do," he states; "trim my whiskers." I trim them, oh, very carefully. They hang augustly down over his black stole. I gaze at him, entranced, and at his portrait painted by a young artist. "I think you have caught the spirit of the ideal," he admitted. "Put me on the mantel." I obey him.[1]

---

[1] Oh, ladies and gentlemen, patient sitters for portraits, what if the puppets do reverse the usual order of things? Must you not envy them? Think of having your portrait painted first, the portrait of the *ideal you* by an artist, and then having a complaisant Creator fashioning your features into the nearest possible semblance of what you might wish to be! Think of it. How delightful for you and how simple for the portrait painter!

Next I take up the Spy. He writhes in my hand. I ply the paint brush, more yellow paint on the yellow spots. True to prediction, his strings become entangled. "I told you so," hissed the green and yellow Spy. "My spots will dry over night. You must arrange my strings tomorrow." I set him beside the Chief Prophet where he slinks down and subsides. "Hee, hee, hee," snickers the other Spy who has cerise spots of silk on lavender. He is crouched on the floor in a heap. I raise him and place him beside his fellow. He reaches out a long brown arm and pokes him slyly.

I collect the other dolls. Very crude little rag affairs they seem in their unfinished condition. The naked, white body of the King I lay beside that of the Sentinel. One could scarcely tell them apart except that the feet of the King are already encased in little scarlet boots which are long and pointed and curled at the tips. The King is a stiff, unbending person. But the other is a well built fellow fashioned with exceeding care to stand and walk and sit superbly in a few clothes holding a long red spear and a shield. Into the box I lay them, white bodies, blank faces, limber arms and legs. "I shall have to shop again for the King's purple robe. What a bore!" I think, as I dump disjointed priests, children and servants, all on top of His Majesty, and close the cover of the tin box.

"You are insolent," said the Chief Prophet of the Stars. "Well, yes, perhaps, oh mighty marionette," I admit, "but I am sleepy. Goodnight."

"Fatigue is human," remarked the black-robed Priest. "We marionettes transcend such frailty." "We are immortal!!!" boomed forth the Chief Prophet. "So saith Anatole France, also Charles Magnin, also others." "Hist," whispered one of the Spies, "it is written in *The Mask*. . . ." And, as I moved quietly about in the adjoining room I heard them discussing many matters, concerning themselves, of course. There was talk of the ancient Indian Ramajana, of the Joruri plays of Japan, of bleeding Saints and nodding Madonnas in Mediaeval churches. The conversation veered to Pulcinella, his kinship with Kasper and Karagheuz and with Punch across the channel. There were murmurings of the names of Goethe, Voltaire, even Shakespeare to say nothing of Bernard Shaw, Maeterlinck, Hoffmansthal, Schnitzler, all from the dolls on the mantel and much, much more besides. Some things I overheard distinctly before I fell asleep: some I may have dreamed. All that I could recall I have put into a little book.

Puppets of Antiquity

> "I wish to discant on the marionette.
> One needs a keen taste for it and also a little veneration.
> The marionette is august; it issues from a sanctuary . . ."
> ANATOLE FRANCE

PERHAPS the most impressive approach to the marionettes is through the trodden avenue of history. If we travel from distant antiquity where the first articulated idols were manipulated by ingenious, hidden devices in the vast temples of India and Egypt, if we follow the footprints of the puppets through classic centuries of Greece and Rome and trace them even in the dark ages of early Christianity whence they emerged to wander all over mediaeval Europe, in the cathedrals, along the highways, in the market places and at the courts of kings, we may have more understanding and respect for the quaint little creatures we find exhibited crudely in the old, popular manner on the street corner or presented, consciously naïve and precious, upon the art stage of an enthusiastic younger generation. For the marionette has a history. No human race can boast a longer or more varied, replete with such high dignities and shocking indignities, romantic adventure and humble routine, triumphs, decadences, revivals. No human race has explored so many curious corners of the earth, adapted itself to the characteristic tastes of such diverse peoples and, nevertheless, retained its essential, individual traits through ages of changing environment and ideals.

The origin of the puppet is still somewhat of a mystery, dating back, as it undoubtedly does, to the earliest stages of the very oldest civilizations. Scholars differ as to the birthplace and ancestry. Professor Richard Pischel, who has made an exhaustive study of this phase of the subject, believes that the puppet came into being along with fairy tales on the banks of the Ganges, "in the old wonderland of India." The antiquity of the Indian marionette, indeed, is attested by the very legends of the national deities. It was the god Siva who fell in love with the beautiful puppet of his wife Parvati. The most ancient marionettes were made of wool, wood, buffalo horn and ivory; they seem to have been popular with adults as well as with children. In an old, old collection of Indian tales, there is an account of a basketful of marvellous wooden dolls presented by the daughter of a celebrated mechanician to a princess. One of these could be made to fly through the air by pressing a wooden peg, another to dance, another to talk! Large talking puppets were even introduced upon the stage with living actors. An old Sanskrit drama has been found in which they took part. But in India real puppet shows, themselves, seem to have antedated the regular drama, or so we may infer from the names given to the director of the actors, which is *Sutradhara* (Holder of the Strings) and to the stage manager, who is called *Sthapaka* (Setter up). The implication naturally is that these two important functionaries of the oldest Indian drama took their titles from the even more ancient and previously established puppet plays.

There are authorities, however, who consider Egypt the original birthplace of the marionette, among these *Yorick* (P. Ferrigni), whose vivid history of puppets is accessible in various issues of *The Mask*. Yorick claims that the marionette originated somehow with the aborigines of the Nile and that before the days of Manete who founded Memphis, before the Pharaohs, great idols moved their hands and opened their mouths, inspiring worshipful terror in the hearts of the beholders. Dr. Berthold Laufer corroborates this opinion. He maintains that marionettes first appeared in Egypt and Greece, and spread from there to all countries of Asia. The tombs of ancient Thebes and Memphis have yielded up many small painted puppets of ivory and wood, whose limbs can be moved by pulling a string. These are figures of beasts as well as of men and they may have been toys. Indeed, it is often claimed that puppets are descended, not from images of the gods, but from "the first doll that was ever put into the hands of a child."

The *Boston Transcript*, in 1904, published a report of an article by A. Gayet in *La Revue* which gives a minute description of a marionette theatre excavated at Antinoë. There, in the tomb of Khelmis, singer of Osiris, archaeologists have unearthed a little Nile galley or barge of wood with a cabin in the centre and two ivory doors that open to reveal a stage. A rod across the front of this stage is supported by two uprights and from this rod light wires were found still hanging. Other indications leave little doubt that this miniature theatre was used in a religious rite, possibly on the anniversary of the death of the god Osiris, whose father was Ra, the sun, as a sort of passion play performed by puppets before an audience of the initiated. Mortuary paintings show us the ritual and tell us the story. As everything excavated at this site is reported to be of the Roman or Coptic period this is probably the oldest marionette theatre ever discovered!

The Chinese puppets and still older *shadows* of the land as well as of other Oriental countries are all of considerable antiquity. In truth, it matters little whence came the first of the puppets, from India, Egypt or from China, nor how descended, from the idols of priests or the playthings of children. It is enough to know of their indisputably ancient lineage and the honorable position granted them in the legends of gods and heroes. Whatever remains uncertain or fantastic in the theories of their origin can only add to the aura of romance surrounding this imperishable race of fragile beings.

In the mythology of the Greeks one may find mention of the august ancestors of the marionettes. Passages in the Iliad describe the marvellous golden tripods fashioned by Vulcan which moved of themselves. A host of great articulated idols were to be found in the temples all over Greece. These were moved, Charles Magnin avers, by various devices such as quicksilver, leadstone, springs, etc. There was Jupiter Ammon, borne upon the shoulders of the priests, who indicated with his head the direction he wished to travel. There were the Apollo of Heliopolis, the Theban Venus, the statues created by Daedalus and many others, all manipulated by priests from within the hollow bodies.

But aside from these inspiring deities, in fact right along with them, Greek puppetry grew up and flourished. Yorick writes, "Greece from remotest times of which any accounts have come down to us had marionette theatres in the public places of all the most populated cities. She had famous showmen whose names, recorded on the pages of the most illustrious writers, have triumphed over death and oblivion. She had her 'balletti' and pantomimes exclusively conceived and preordained for the play of 'pupazzi,' etc." Eminent mathematicians interested themselves in perfecting the mechanism of the dolls until, as Apuleius wrote, "Those who direct the movement of the little wooden figures have nothing else to do but to pull the string of the member they wish to set in motion and immediately the head bends, the eyes turn, the hands lend themselves to any action and the elegant little person moves and acts as though

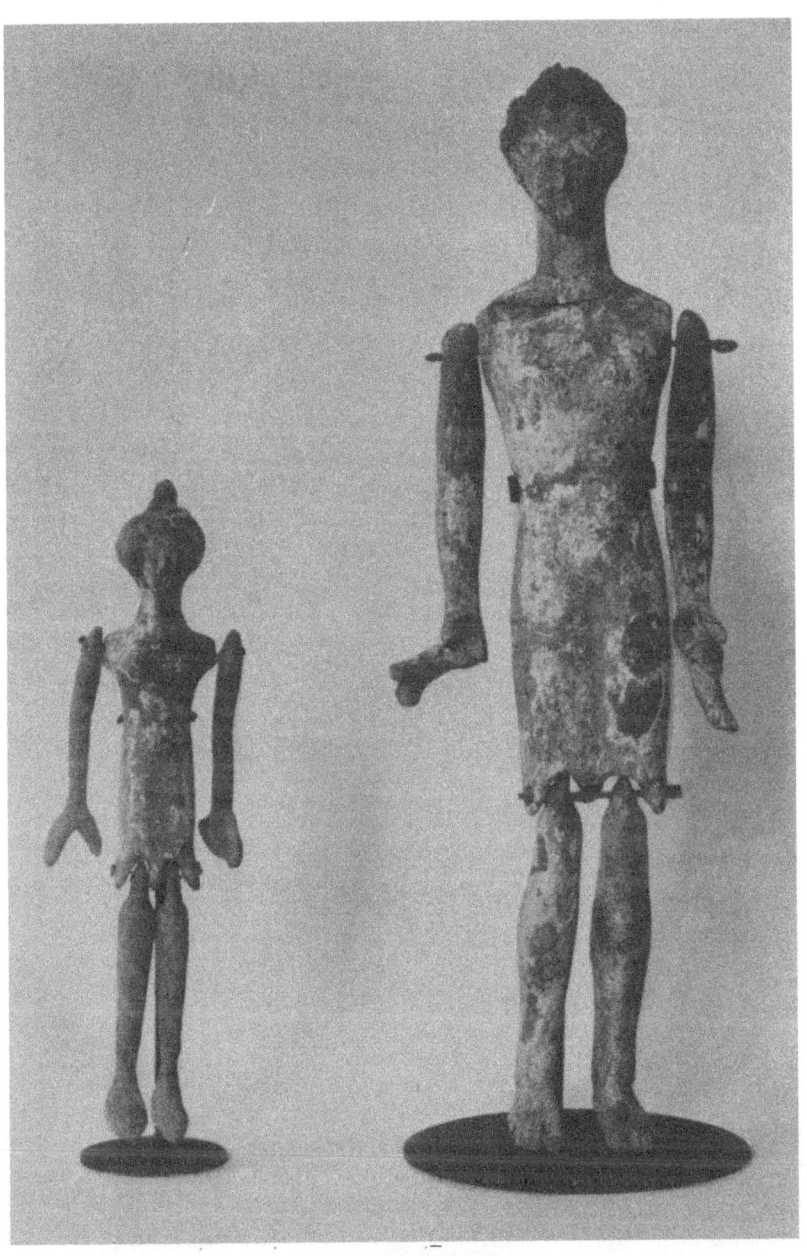

JOINTED DOLLS OR PUPPETS
Terra-cotta, probably Attic
[Courtesy of the Museum of Fine Arts, Boston]

MARIONETTES

it were alive." A pleasant hyperbole of Apuleius perhaps, but some of us credulously prefer to have faith in it.

In the writings of the celebrated Heron of Alexandria, living two centuries before Christ, one can find a very minute description of a puppet show for which he planned the ingenious mechanism. He explains that there were two kinds of automata, first those acting on a movable stage which itself advanced and retreated at the end of the acts and second, those performing on a stationary stage divided into acts by a change of scene. The *Apotheosis of Bacchus* was of the first type, the action presented within a miniature temple wherein stood the statue of the god with dancing bacchantes circling around, fountains jetting forth milk, garlands of flowers, sounding cymbals, all accomplished by a mechanism of weights and cords. It was an extremely elaborate affair. Of the second type of puppet show Heron cites as example *The Tragedy of Nauplius*, the mechanism for which was invented by a contemporary engineer, Philo of Byzantium. There were five scenes disclosed, one after the other, by doors which opened and closed: first, the seashore, with workmen constructing the ships, hammering, sawing, etc.; second, the coast with the Greeks dragging their ships to the water; third, sky and sea, with the ships sailing over the waters which begin to grow rough and stormy; fourth, the coast of Euboë, Nauplius brandishing a torch on the rocks and shoals whither the Greek vessels steer and are shattered (Athene stands behind Nauplius, who is the instrument of her vengeance); fifth, the wreck of the ships, Ajax struggling and drowning in the waves, Athene appearing in a thunder clap! This play was probably taken from episodes of the Homeric legend and, although Heron does not so state, the action of the puppets was most likely accompanied by a recital of the poem upon which the drama was founded.

Xenophon describes still another type of show, a banquet at which the host brought in a Syracusan juggler to amuse the guests with his dancing marionettes. The best showmen in Greece seem to have been Sicilians. These peripatetic showmen went from town to town with their figures in a box. The plays they presented were generally keen, strong satires on the foibles of human nature, the vices of the times, the prominent or pompous persons of the day, parodies on popular dramas or schools of philosophy. They were a favorite diversion of the masses and of cultured people as well. Even Socrates is reported to have bandied words with a Sicilian showman, asking him how he made a living in his profession. To which the showman made reply: "The folly of men is an inexhaustible fund of riches and I am always sure of filling my purse by moving a few pieces of wood." Eventually the puppets usurped a place upon the classic stage itself, and it is reported that a puppet player, Potheinus, had a small stage specially erected for his marionettes on the thymele of the

MARIONETTES 21

great theatre of Dionysius at Athens where Euripedes' plays had been presented.

The Romans borrowed marionette traditions from the Greeks as they did many other art forms. There were large articulated statues of the gods and emperors in Rome. At Praeneste the celebrated group of the infants of Jupiter and Juno seated upon the knees of Fortune appears to have been of this sort; the nurse seems to have been movable. Livy describes a banquet celebration and the terror of the people and of the Senate upon hearing that the gods averted their heads from the dishes presented them. Ovid, also, gives an account of the startling effect produced upon the beholders when the statue of Servus Tullius moved. As in Greece, there were special puppet performances given in private homes as well as the wandering shows along the highways. The latter were popular with common people, with poets, philosophers and emperors. Marcus Aurelius wrote about them, Horace and Persius mentioned them.

The personages of the Roman puppet stage generally represented obvious and amusing types of humanity; their repertoire consisted chiefly of bold satire and parodies on popular dramas. The conventionalized characters of Roman marionette theatres were not at all dissimilar from the later heroes of the Italian *fantoccini*. A bronze portrait of Maccus, the Roman buffoon, which was unearthed in

1727, might serve almost as a statue of Pulcinella, hooked nose, nut-cracker chin, hunchback and all. In fact it is thought that these Roman mimes or *sanni* have lived on in the Italian *burattini*, and in the characters of the Commedia dell' Arte. This theory has been criticized by some who feel that the *personaggi* such as Arlecchino and Pulcinella grew out of the mannerisms and characteristics of the Italians, just as the puppet buffoons of Rome were true offspring of the Roman people, and that any resemblances between them may be laid at the door of common frailties existing in humanity of all ages and ever fit subject for the satirical play of puppets. Nevertheless it is not impossible to believe that through the curiously confused period in Italy when Pagan culture was giving way to Christianity, when heathen ideals were half perishing, half persisting, something of the old was embodied in, assimilated with the new. And so it may have happened with the marionettes, Maccus emerging with much of Pulcinella, Citeria appearing as Columbine. We have Pappus Bruccus and Casnar, the parasite, the glutton, the fool, passed on somehow.

But not alone this. Excavators in the Catacombs have discovered small jointed puppets of ivory or wood in many tombs. They look like dolls, but they may have been religious images used by the earliest Christians. The Iconoclasts in their zeal annihilated everything that had the appearance of an idol, and many a puppet perished along with the images

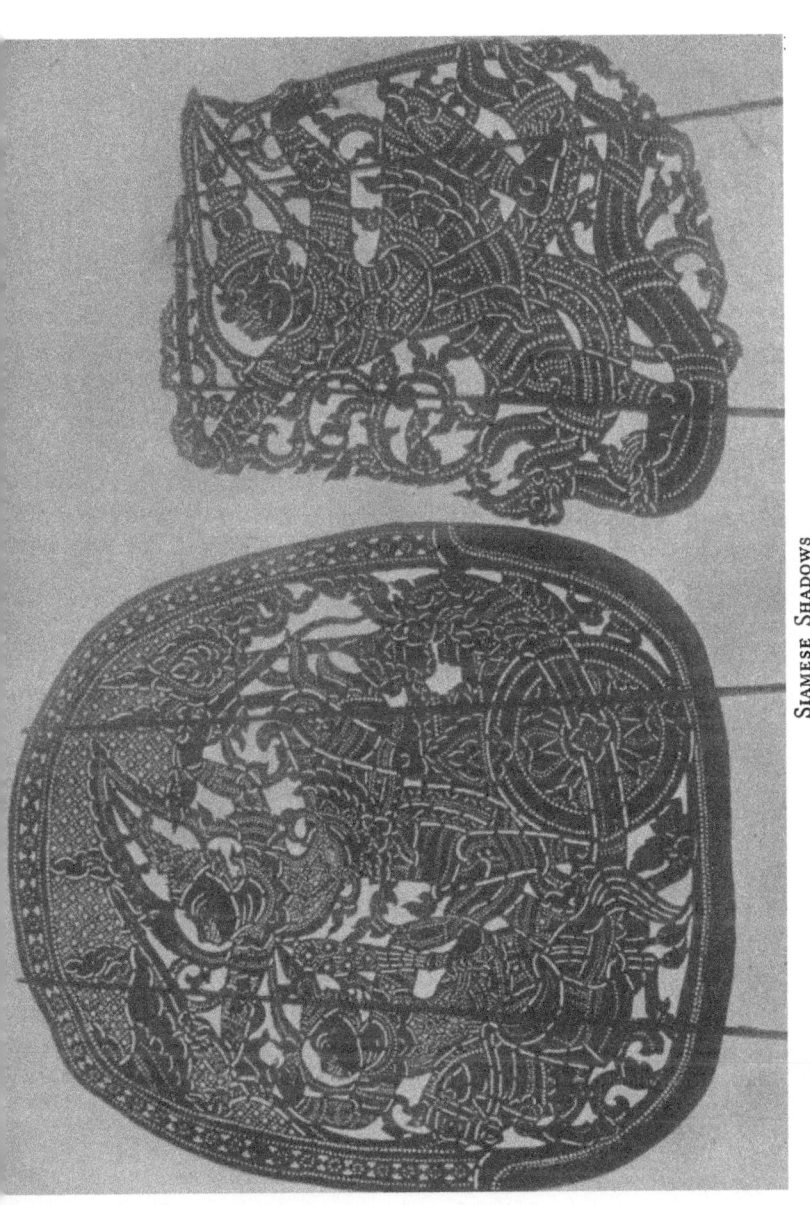

SIAMESE SHADOWS
Belonging to the collection in the Smithsonian Institution, U. S. National Museum. This collection was presented by the King of Siam in 1876

of the gods, Maccus as well as Apollo! But soon the Church saw the wisdom of using concrete, vivid representation instead of mere abstract symbolism scarcely comprehensible to the simple minded. "Into the churches crept figures, Jesus' body on the Cross instead of the Lamb. To the Apollo of Heliopolis succeeded the crucifix of Nicodemus, to the Theban Venus the Madonna of Orihuela." (P. Ferrigni.) Occasionally these figures were made to move a head or to gesticulate. And here we find the earliest beginnings of the mysteries which were later to come out from the churches and monasteries as precursors not only of our puppet shows but of practically all our drama.

Oriental Puppets

THERE are few of us who at times have not unleashed our imaginations, flung away the reins and bidden our thoughts roam freely beyond the vision of our straining eyes. Who has not pondered whimsically what sort of crooked creatures may be shambling over the craters and crevices of the moon? Similarly the unfamiliar Eastern lands afford adventure for our Western fancies. How alluring the imaginary sights and sounds fantastically flavored; glimmer of spangles, daggers, veils and turbans, camels and busy bazaars and mosques white in the sun, strumming of curious instruments, gurgle, clatter and patter, enigmatical whisperings and silences of unknown import. But of all things so strange what could be fashioned stranger than the puppets of Eastern peoples? As the dreams and philosophies of the Orient seem farther away from us than its most distant cities, so these small symbols of unfamiliar creeds and cultures for us are most amazing. What skill and artistry is displayed in the creation of them, what capricious imagery in their conception! Let us consider them.

Probably the Javanese *shadows* present the most weirdly fascinating spectacle to our unaccustomed

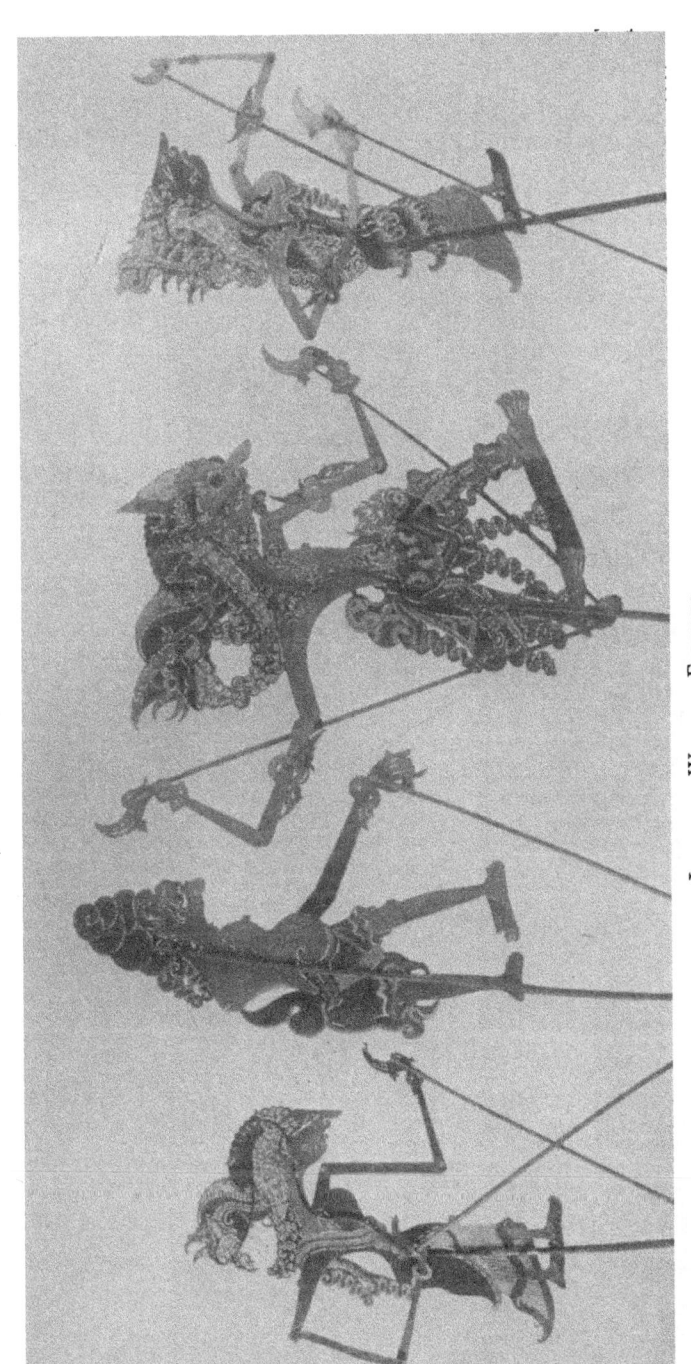

JAVANESE WAYANG FIGURES
[American Museum of Natural History, New York]

eyes. What singular creatures are here? Bizarre beyond all description, grotesque forms with long, lean beckoning arms and incredible profiles, adorned with curious, elaborate ornamentation. They are made of buffalo skin, carefully selected, ingeniously treated, intricately cut and chiseled, richly gilded and cunningly colored, and they are supported and manipulated by fragile and graceful rods of horn or bamboo. Such are the colorful and inscrutable little figures of gods and heroes in the *Wayang Purwa*, ancient and celebrated drama of Java, popular now as in the days of Java's independence.

These shadow-plays are half mythical and religious, half heroic and national in character, portraying the well-known feats of native gods and princes, the battles of their royal armies, their miraculous and preposterous adventures with giants and other fabulous creatures. Each incident, each character is familiar to the audience. One heroine is thus described in Javanese poetry. "She was really a flower of song, the virgin in the house of Pati. She was petted by her father. Her well-proportioned figure was in perfect accord with her skill in working. She was acquainted with the secrets of literature. She used the Kawi speech fluently, as she had practised it from childhood. She was elegant in the recitation of formulas of belief and never neglected the five daily prayer hours. She was truly Godfearing. Moreover, she never forgot her batik work. She wove gilded passementerie and painted it with figures, etc., etc. She was truly queen of the accomplished, neat and charming in her manner, sweet and light in her gestures, etc., etc.

"She was sprayed with rosewater. Her body was warm and hot if not anointed every hour. She was the virgin in the house of Pati. Everyone who saw her loved her. She had only one fault. Later, when she married, she could not endure a rival mistress. She was jealous, etc."

A prose account tells us of the same young lady. It is said of Kyahi Pati Logender's youngest child: "This was a daughter called Andjasmara, beautiful of form. If one wished to do full justice to her appearance the describer would certainly grow weary before all of her beauty could be portrayed. She was charming, elegant, sweet, talkative, lovely, etc., etc. Happy he who should obtain her as a wife."

The plots are based upon old, old Indian saga, from the *Mahabharata*, the *Ramayana*, the *Pandji* legends and also upon native fable such as the *Manik Muja*. There are several varieties of Wayang play, each founded upon one or several of these sources. The *Wayang Purwa* and the *Wayang Gedog* are silhouette plays presented by leather figures behind a lighted screen. Sometimes, however, the women in the audience are seated on one side of the screen, the men on the other, so that some see the gray shadows, others the colored figures. The *Wayang* Keletik is given not with shadows but with the painted hide figures themselves displayed to the audience. All these per-

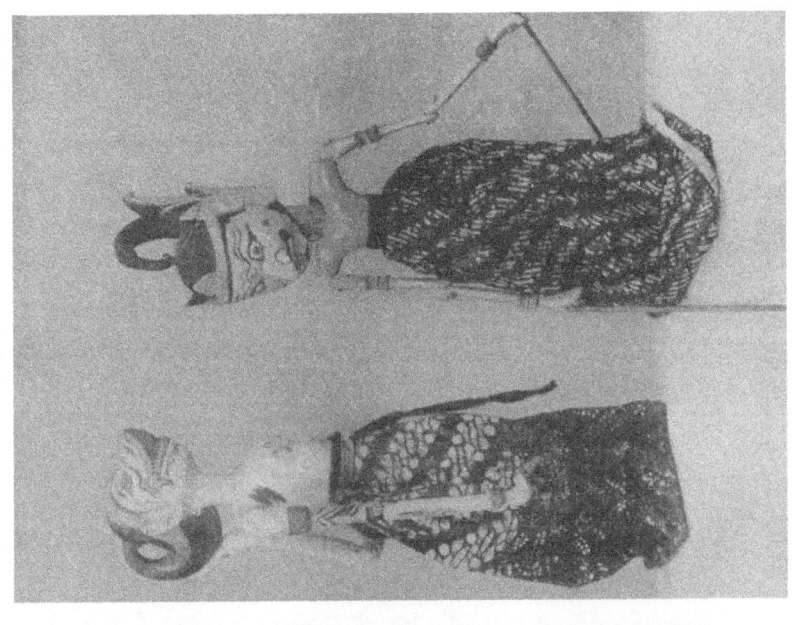
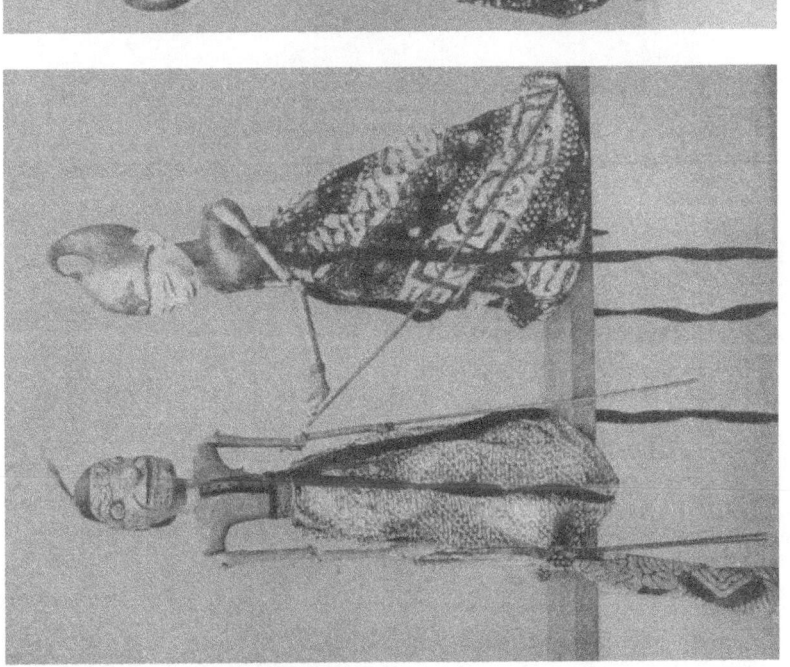

JAVANESE ROUNDED MARIONETTES
[American Museum of Natural History, New York]

formances are not ordinary public events, but rather special productions in celebration of particular occasions. Etiquette at the Wayang demands that regular rites be observed before the performance, incense burned and food offered to the gods.

The *Dalang*, or showman, is a person of great skill and versatility. He seats himself cross-legged on a mat surrounded by figures; there are about one hundred and twenty to a complete Wayang set. He directs the gamelin music of the orchestra which keeps up a tomtom and scraping of catgut throughout, gives a short preliminary exposition of the plot, brings on the characters which he holds and manipulates with slender rods, places them with precision and then the play begins. The Dalang, as the music softens, speaks for each one of the characters. The general tone is heroic with comedy introduced upon occasion. There are struggles, battles, love scenes, dances. The Dalang shuffles with his feet for the dancing, makes a noise of tramping or fighting, adjusts the lights on the screen, all the while moving the figures and speaking feelingly for them.

Besides these so-called shadows the Javanese have also rounded marionettes carved out of wood, which have long, slender arms and fantastic touches revealing kinship with the figures of painted hide. The play presented by these crude but rather startling dolls is called *Wayang Golek*. The puppets are moved from below by rods attached to their bodies and hands as are the shadow figures. Still other types of plays are the *Wayang Beber*, presented by rolls of pictures, and much later (eighteenth century) the *Wayang Topang* in which rigidly trained human actors, dressed in the conventional costumes of the Wayang figures, take the parts of the puppets. But here as in the puppet dramas the Dalang reads all the words.

On the island of Bali, one of the group of the Indian Archipelago, Wayang plays are like those of Java. The old figures are very wonderful, cut out of young buffalo hide, carefully treated and prepared. The tool formerly used to make them was a primitive pointed knife. The Wayang sets made to-day, in spite of the superiority of modern European instruments which are employed, are very crude in comparison. This is because with the loss of independence the natives also lost all interest in their own art and culture; indeed new Wayangs are made only when the old ones are worn out.

The shadows of the Siamese *Nang* are also unusual. This is a representation of certain scenes from the Indian epic, *Ramayana*, and depicts the adventures of Prince Rama and his wife Sita. It is given in private homes for special festivals and is of a serious, poetic nature. As described by a native of Siam, "It is a show of moving, transparent pictures over a screen illumined by a strong bonfire behind." It is recited by two readers and sometimes requires as many as twenty operators. The figures more nearly approach the human form than do those of the Java-

MARIONETTES

nese shadows, but their queer, pointed headdress and strange costuming produce a very striking and highly stylized effect. They are made of hide which has been previously cut, scraped and stretched with extreme care. The technique of decorating the figures is most difficult, for the forms are stenciled and perforated by an infinite number of pricks, to indicate not only the outlines but also the nature of the fabric of garments, the jewels, weapons, etc. These perforations scarcely show unless held before a light, when they give a very rich and variegated effect. There is great art as well in the dyeing and fixing of the colors, and in estimating the amount of light which should be allowed to penetrate so as to give a well-proportioned aspect to the figure as a whole. In Siam as in Java there are to be found ordinary dramatic performances by wooden puppets more recent in origin and not unlike those of Burma.

These puppet theatres of Burma exhibit a peculiar combination of fantastic legend and grotesque, realistic humor. The puppet stage of the country seems to have been more highly developed than its regular drama. A visiting company of Burmese marionettes was displayed at the Folies Bergères in Paris, where they were much admired for their beautiful costumes, wonderful technical construction, the natural poses they assumed and the graceful gestures they made. Mr. J. Arthur MacLean tells of the annual celebration which he witnessed a few years ago at

Ananda, the famous old Buddhist site. It consisted of a performance by the temple puppets which began early in the evening and lasted all the night through. The marionettes were the property of the temple and when not in use were stored away there. They were large and elaborate and manipulated with strings. The audience comprised the entire population of the village; every man and woman was present and they had brought all of their children. The first part of the show was comical for the sake of the children who, we may presume, fell asleep as the night progressed. The plays which followed became more and more serious and were of a religious nature. Some Burmese puppets, however, are very primitive, being painted wooden dolls, odd and humorous in spirit. The license of the showman is extreme, but does not seem to offend the taste of the native audience.

In Turkestan and in Central Asia puppet shows are a very popular diversion along with the feats of jugglers and dancers. There are two types of puppets existing, one the very diminutive dolls carried about by ambulant players whose extremely naïve dialogue is composed chiefly for the amusement of children. The other, on a larger scale, is to be seen on small stages erected in coffee houses or at weddings and other private celebrations.

R. S. Rehm gives a description of a crude little marionette theatre in Samarkand. Out in the crowded narrow streets sounds as terrifying as the

BURMESE PUPPETS
Upper: Made of rag, cotton and plaster
Lower: Made of painted wood
[American Museum of Natural History, New York]

MARIONETTES

trumpet on the walls of Jericho announced the beginning of the performance. The interior was a dark hall with a roof of straw matting through the holes of which mischievous youngsters were continually peeking until they were chased away. It was called *Tschadar Chajal*, Tent of Fantasy. The puppets revealed Indian origin, but their huge heads, with the clothing merely hung upon them, indicated Russian influences. There was one scene of modern warfare with toy cannons hauled upon the stage. Then came a play within a play. Yassaul, the native buffoon, was a sort of master of ceremonies. Various comical and grotesque marionettes appeared whom he greeted and led to their places. The King himself entered upon a miniature horse, dismounted and seated himself on a throne in the tiny audience. The performance for His Majesty consisted of puppet dancers, puppet jugglers and last of all, a marionette representing a drunken European dragged away by a native policeman. At this point the small and also the large audience expressed great delight.

Of the puppets of Persia a very ancient legend tells us how a Chinese shadow play was performed before Ogotai, successor of Tamerlane. The artist presented upon his screen the figure of a turbaned old man being dragged along tied to the tail of a horse. When Ogotai inquired what this might signify the showman is said to have replied: "It is one of the rebellious Mohammedans whom the soldiers are bringing in from the cities in this manner." Whereupon Ogotai, instead of being angry at the taunt, had his Persian art treasures, jewels and rich brocades brought forth, also rare Chinese fabrics and carven stones. Displaying them all to the showman, he pointed out the beauties in the products of both lands as well as the natural difference between them. The showman having learned this lesson of tolerance went away greatly abashed.

Shadows are mentioned in the works of the Persian poet, Muhammed Assar, in 1385, when they seem to have been eagerly cultivated. Since then, however, they have sadly deteriorated. It is said that wandering jugglers with their primitive dolls scarcely elicit a smile from the educated Persians, although they are sometimes asked into homes to amuse guests or children. As a rule they play in open places and after the show the owner collects the pennies from the audience standing around, calling down the curse of Allah upon those who walk away without paying. The comic puppet, according to Karl Friederich Flögel, is Ketschel, a bald-headed hero "more cultured than all the Hanswursts in the world." He spouts poetry, quotes from the Koran, sings of the houris in Paradise and, when alone, throws aside his wisdom, dances and gets drunk.

Professor Pischel has written that he believes the puppet plays of India not only to have antedated the regular drama, but also to have outlived it. He

CINGALESE PUPPETS
Upper: Devil and Merchant
Lower: King and Queen
Part of a collection received from the Ceylon Commission of the
World's Columbian Exposition, 1895, by the Smithsonian
Institution. U. S. National Museum

MARIONETTES

claims moreover that the puppet shows are the only form of dramatic expression left at the present time. What a contribution from the marionette to the land of its birth and, on the other hand, how much the races of India must have given of themselves and their imaginations to the little wooden creatures; for the interest of the beholder, alone, is the breath of life which animates them through the centuries.

It is amusing to read of the life-sized walking and talking puppets used in the tenth century by a dramatist, Rajah Gekhara. One doll represented Sita and another her sister. A starling trained to speak Prakrit was placed in the mouth of *Sita* to speak for her. The puppet player spoke for the other doll as well as for the demon, which part in the drama he himself enacted and spoke in Sanskrit.[1] In one of the issues of *The Mask* there is printed the following account of religious puppets of the thirteenth century in Ceylon. A great festival was being solemnized in the temple, which had been richly decorated for the event and furnished "with numerous images of Brahma dancing with parasols in their hands that were moved by instruments; with moving images of gods of divers forms that went to and fro with their joined hands raised in adoration; with moving figures of horses prancing; . . . with likenesses of great elephants . . . with these and divers other shows did

[1] Only the principal male parts were allowed to speak Sanskrit according to the conventions of Hindu dramaturgy. Lesser male and all female parts were spoken in Prakrit.

he make the temple exceeding attractive." (Mahavamsa, ch. 85).

In quite recent days, P. C. Jinavaravamsa, himself a priest and prince of Siam, as well as an artist, has written an article attesting the aesthetic worth and popularity of Indian puppets to-day. "Beautiful figures, six to eight inches high, representing the characters of the Indian drama, *Ramayana*, are made for exhibition at royal entertainments. They are perfect pieces of mechanism; their very fingers can be made to grasp an object and they can be made to assume postures expressive of any action or emotion described in poetry; this is done by pulling strings which hang down within the clothing or within a small tube attached to the lower part of the figure, with a ring or a loop attached to each, for inserting the fingers of the showman. The movements are perfectly timed to the music and recitation of singing. One cannot help being charmed by these Lilliputs, whose dresses are so gorgeous and jeweled with the minutest detail. Little embroidered jackets and other pieces of dress, representing magnificent robes of a Deva or Yakha, are complete in the smallest particular; the miniature jewels are sometimes made of real gold and gems."

The popular plays of India have never been written down, as were the classic dramas, but, according to the custom of wandering showmen, they were handed on from father to son. Thus, much in them has been lost for us. But Vidusaka, the buffoon, has survived,

EAST INDIAN PUPPETS

From an old rest house for pilgrims connected with an old Jain Temple at Ahmadabad. The figures were attached to a mechanical organ and their motions followed the music

[Part of a collection in the Brooklyn Institute Museum]

MARIONETTES

"as old as the oldest Indian art," the fundamental type of comic character, and possibly the prototype of them all, — Vidusaka, a hunchbacked dwarf with protruding teeth, a Brahmin with a bald head and distorted visage. He excites merriment by his acts, his dress, his figure and his speech. He is quarrelsome, gluttonous, stupid, vain, cowardly, insolent and pugnacious, "always ready to lay about him with a stick." Professor Pischel avers that we can follow this little comedian as he wandered away with the gypsy showmen whose original home was that of the marionette, mysterious ancient India. He trails him into Turkey, where he became metamorphosed into the famous (or infamous) Karagheuz after having served as a model for the buffoons of Persia, Arabia and Egypt. But more than this, it is believed that long before Arlecchino and other offspring of Maccus found their way northward there existed in the mystery and carnival plays of Germany a funny fellow with all the family traits of the descendants of the Indian Vidusaka. And it was probably the gypsies again, coming up from Persia and Turkey through the Balkan countries and Hungary (where similar types of puppet-clowns are to be discovered) who carried the cult from far-off times and introduced into Austria and Germany the ancient ancestor of Hanswurst and Kasperle.

In Turkey, as in so many Oriental countries, the shadow play is the chief representative of dramatic art. There are several little tales told concerning the origin of Turkish puppets. One relates how a Sultan, long ago, commanded his Vizier on pain of death to bring back to life two favorite court fools whom he had executed, perhaps somewhat rashly. The Vizier, in this dire dilemma, consulted with a wise Dervish, who thereupon caught two fish, skinned them and cut out of the dried skins two figures representing the two dead jesters. These he displayed to the Sultan behind a lighted curtain, and the illusion seems to have satisfied that autocratic personage.

Another story tells that long ago in Stamboul there lived a good man who grieved daily with righteous indignation over the misrule of the governing Pashas. He pondered long how to improve conditions and how to carry the matter to the attention of the Sultan himself. Finally he decided to establish a shadow play whose fame, he hoped, might lure the Sultan in to see it. And, indeed, the people thronged to witness his Karagheuz. But when at last the august Sultan came and took his place in the audience, Karagheuz had more serious matters to display than his usual pranks. The Sultan's eyes were opened to the abuses of his ministers, whom he removed and justly punished. The founder of the Karagheuz play, on the other hand, was made Vizier. His show has remained the favorite diversion of the people.

These Turkish shadows are all centered around the hero, a sort of native Don Juan, a scamp with a

TURKISH SHADOW FIGURE OF KARAGHEUZ
[From Georg Jacob's *Das Schattentheater*]

MARIONETTES 37

good bit of mother wit; he is called "Karagheuz" (Black Eye). There are about sixty other characters to a complete cast, among them Hadji-aivat, representative of the cultured classes and boon companion of Karagheuz, and Bekri Mustafa, the rich peasant just come to town, who frequents questionable resorts, gets drunk and is invariably plundered. There are Kawassan, the rich Jew, and a Dervish and a romantic robber and the Frank and the wife and daughter of Hadji-aivat and all sorts of dancers, beggar-women, etc. George Jacob brings to notice also pathological types such as the dwarf, the opium fiend, the stutterer and others; also representatives of foreign nations, the Arabian, the Persian, the Armenian, the Jew, the Greek, all of whose peculiar accents and mistakes in speaking the Turkish language form a constant source of merriment to the Turks themselves. The plot generally consists of the improper adventures of Karagheuz, his tricks to secure money, his surprising indecencies, his broad, satirical comment on the life about him. Théophile Gautier was present at a Karagheuz performance. He writes: "It is impossible to give in our language the least idea of these huge jests, these hyperbolical, broad jokes which necessitate to render them the dictionary of Rabelais, of Beroalde of Eutrapel flanked by the vulgar catechism of Vade."

The extreme beauty of the production, however, and the expertness of the manipulator somewhat redeem the performances for our Western eyes. The figures are cut out of camelskin, the limbs skilfully articulated. Holes in the necks or chests and, for special figures which gesticulate, also in the hands, enable slender rods to be inserted at right angles by which they are manipulated. The appearance of the transparent, brightly colored figures, with heavy exaggerated outlines, rather resembles mosaic work, while the faces are sometimes done with the extreme care of portraits. The effect produced by these luminous forms is truly beautiful; the color is heightened by surrounding darkness, which tends to increase the seeming size of the figures and to give them an almost plastic quality.

From an account of F. von Luschan we may imagine the usual Karagheuz performance to take place in somewhat the following manner. In any coffee house the rear corner is screened off with a thick curtain into which is inserted a frame. Over the frame a linen is stretched taut. Behind it is set a platform or table upon or at which the operator places himself and his figures. There is little equipment. Four oil lamps with several wicks are furnished with good olive oil to distribute an even illumination behind the screen. The manipulator brings on his characters and talks for them. If two of them gesticulate simultaneously, he overcomes the difficulty by holding one of the rods lightly pressed against his body, thus freeing a hand for the emergency. He must also keep time to the dancing with his castanets, stamp the floor for marching, smack himself loudly to imitate

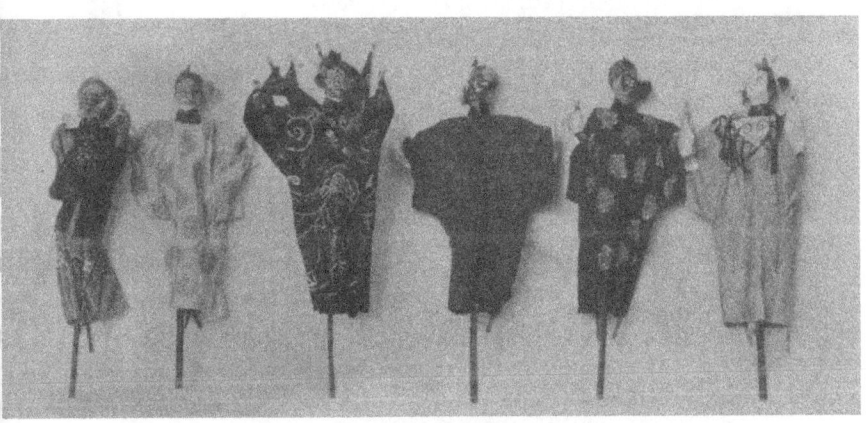

CHINESE PUPPETS
Upper: Operated from above with strings
Lower: Operated from below with sticks
[American Museum of Natural History, New York]

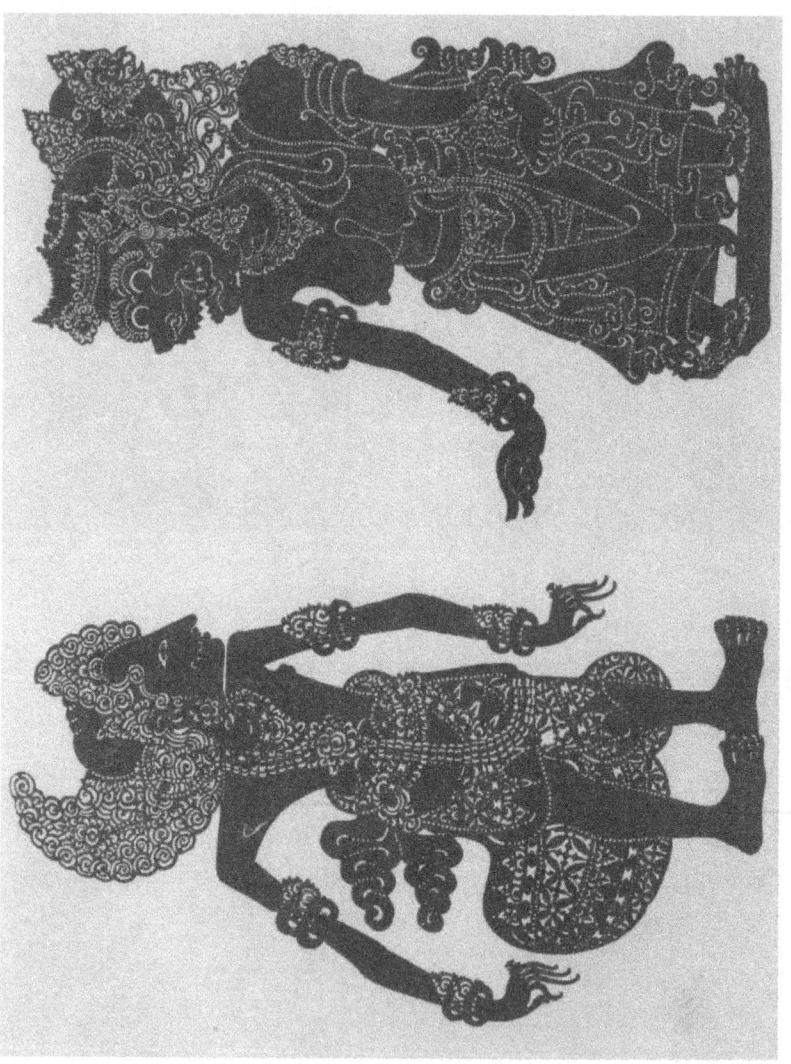

Wayang Figures from the Island of Bali
[Collected by and belonging to Mr. Maurice Sterne, New York]

MARIONETTES

the sound of buffets and keep an eye on the lamps which threaten constantly to set fire to himself and his paraphernalia.

These Karagheuz shows are popular not only throughout Turkey but, more or less altered, in Syria, Palestine, Arabia, Egypt, Tunis, Tripoli, and Morocco. It is recorded that in 1557 in Cairo a puppet play was instrumental in stirring up a revolt and had to be prohibited. In Arabia the shadows are decidedly debased in character, crude, and wholly inartistic. In Tunis the performances are said to be mere conglomerations of obscene incidents. Guy de Maupassant writes in his *Vie Errante:* "We must not forget that it was only a very few years ago that the performances of Caragoussa, a kind of obscene Punch and Judy, were forbidden. Children looked on with their large black eyes, some ignorant, others corrupt, laughing and applauding the improbable and vile exploits which are impossible to narrate." In 1842, however, a traveller in Algiers witnessed a shadow play presenting incidents from the *Arabian Nights' Tales*, in which Karagheuz was a less rude buffoon than usual. At the end of the play there appeared upon the screen the illumined inscription: "There is no God but Allah and Mohammed is his Prophet."

In China the art of the shadow play has long, long ago attained a degree of perfection as high if not surpassing that of any other country. The Chinese have quaintly designed marionettes, but in the magical beauty of their shadows they are without peers. It is only within the last few decades, in fact, that the artists of Paris with the shadow plays at the Chat Noir have succeeded in at all approaching their skill and inspiration.

According to legend one might infer, although scholars deem it doubtful, that the origin of puppets in the wide dominions of bygone Emperors, Celestial Ones, dates back to the earliest periods of a remarkably ancient culture. One story relates that a thousand years B.C. shadows had grown so popular and famous that King Muh commanded a famous showman named Yen Sze to come into his palace and amuse him, his wives and concubines. Yen Sze, thus honored, bestirred himself to operate the figures in an animated manner and proceeded to make his little puppets cast admiring glances at the ladies of the Court. The King became jealously enraged and ordered Yen's head chopped off. Poor Yen Sze, — he barely escaped his horrible fate by tearing up his little figures and proving them harmless creatures of leather, glue and varnish. Another fable tells us that in the year 262 B.C. an Emperor of the Han dynasty was being besieged in the City of Ping in the Province of Schensi by the warrior-wife of Mao-Tun, named O. Now the Emperor's adviser, being full of cunning, and having heard of the jealous disposition of the warlike lady O, devised a scheme for ingeniously ridding the Emperor of his enemies. He placed upon the walls of the beleaguered city a gorgeously dressed

Chinese Shadow-play Figures: collected by B. Laufer in Pekin, 1901
[American Museum of Natural History, New York]

MARIONETTES 41

female puppet and by means of hidden strings made her dance alluringly upon the ramparts. Lady O, deceived by the lifelike imitation and fearing, should the city fall, that her husband, Mao-Tun, might fall in love with this seductive dancer, raised the siege and withdrew her armies from the Emperor's City of Ping in the Province of Schensi. So wonderful, so helpful were the puppets of China in 262 B.C.!

In more modern days there are several sorts of Chinese marionettes. In any open place one might come upon the simple, peripatetic showman with a gathering of little bald-headed children around him, (hence, they say, the name Kwo or Mr. Kwo, which means Baldhead). Stepping upon a small platform the puppeteer dons a sort of sheath of blue cotton, like a big bag, tight at the ankles and full higher up. He then places his box on his shoulders with its open stage to the audience. His head is enclosed behind this stage and his hands are thrust into the dresses of the dolls and manipulate them, a finger for each arm. and for the head. The dialogue is rough, realistic humor. When the act is over he places the puppets and sheath in his box and strolls on with the complete outfit under his arm.

In the large stationary marionette theatres a very different state of affairs exists. Here with expensive and elaborate scenery the puppets are capable of presenting highly spectacular faeries in the manner of the later Italian and French fantoccini. The plot is generally the old one of an enchanted princess guarded by a dragon and rescued by a prince; their marriage ceremony furnishes the occasion for the spectacular display. Some dramas of a romantic or historic nature were composed especially for performances at the court of the Emperor. Sir Lytton Putney, first British Ambassador to China, has described the reception accorded him upon his arrival, one event of which was a marionette play. The chief personage in this piece was a little comedian whose antics delighted the court. The marionettes belonged to the Emperor himself, and the very clever manager of the show was a high official in the palace.

It is the Chinese shadows, however, which are most famous and most amazing for their range of subject and variety of appeal. The figures are of translucent hide, stained with great delicacy. The colors glow like jewels when the light shines through them, and the combination of these colors is amazingly beautiful. The repertoire includes anything and everything in the world of the seen and of the unseen; street comedies, happenings of everyday life, heroic legend, fables, historic drama, religious and mystical revelations with all the ghostly fantasy bred of Taoist teachings (metamorphoses and visions of demons marvellously produced!). According to the account of Rehm in his extensive work *Das Buch der Marionetten*, the beauty and power of these fascinating illusions carry the spectator away into realms of make-believe. He has given several enthusiastic descriptions of the productions. The following is one of them:

CHINESE SHADOW-PLAY FIGURES: COLLECTED BY B. LAUFER IN PEKIN, 1901
Entrance to a house; water-wheel and gate to the lower wheel; gate leading to one of the Purgatories
[American Museum of Natural History, New York]

MARIONETTES

"The story is that of a son, sick with longing, who implores the Ruler of the Shadow-world to show him the spirit of his departed mother. One sees a landscape bathed in the magic atmosphere of twilight. In the background there rises a pagoda whose shimmering reflection is mirrored in the calm lake. All is silence and expectancy. The son appears; he makes his respectful obeisance before the hallowed spot and brings his offering. The smoke of the incense rises in small clouds. Suddenly the silver tones of the wonderful Chinese zither are heard and accompanied by its strains the transformation takes place. The pagoda vanishes, luminous circles of color appear out of which the mother emerges. She speaks to her son, who is trembling with awe; she offers him glimpses of a hidden world, comforts and strengthens him. One hears her sigh, recognizes her perturbation by the rising and falling of her breast and the whole expression of her countenance. The beholders are completely under the sway of the ghostly apparition. In the end everything resumes its former aspect, the peace of the night envelops the landscape resting under the silver moonlight. Swans appear upon the lake bathing their white plumage in the cool waters and with this poetic impression the dream-peace is concluded."

In Japanese literature, according to Mr. Henri Joly, one finds the antiquity of the puppet show traced back into the depths of ages. Thus the story runs: Hiriuk was a very ugly child, so his parents cast him adrift in a boat. The boat floated away and was finally stranded on the shore of Nishinomiya where the boy lived and died. After his death, however, his restless spirit caused storms to rise and the fishermen lost their livelihood until a man, Dokun, arrived who built a temple to the Gods, whereupon the sea became smooth and the fish plentiful. After Dokun's death, the inhabitants neglected the temple. Again gales arose and the fish disappeared. Then came another man named Hiakudaiyu and made a doll and brought it to the temple. Then hiding himself he displayed it and called: "I am Dokun, I have come to greet you." Whereupon the sea again became calm and fish again returned. The emperor hearing of it summoned Hiakudaiyu to perform with his show at court, and after witnessing it he exclaimed: "As Japan is God's country, we must, before anything else, entertain the Gods. Let an office be created!" Hiakudaiyu was officially appointed to travel from shrine to shrine about the land carrying the box which contained his puppets. After his death others continued the art. Another writer claims that Dokun was a Shinto priest, but it matters little.

Japan has developed a marionette tradition altogether and amazingly unique. Indeed so powerful a factor has it been that living actors in the classic drama have accepted the conventions of the puppet stage and are trained to the gesture and manner of the ancient marionette. This does not apply, of course,

OLD JAPANESE PUPPET HEADS
From a collection in the Brooklyn Institute Museum
[Founded by Mr. Stewart Culin in Kyoto, 1912]

to the innumerable strolling booths of the Chinese *linen bag* variety, but rather to the renowned and long established stationary theatres for puppets, theatres with exclusive boxes for the select and well-to-do of the audience and ample seating capacity for the common people who visit the show in great numbers.

The dolls are not quite half as tall as a man; they are very realistically conceived and the mimicry of nature is carried into the minutest details. Mr. Joly has published some tracings of parts of these Japanese puppets which indicate how elaborate the inner mechanism must be; a hand in which each joint of each finger is articulated, a head in which the eyes move from side to side. Indeed, these marionettes frequently raise their eyebrows to express scorn or surprise. The costumes are of rich silk and brocade, profusely embroidered, often jeweled and always designed with special thought for their decorative effect. Nay more, when a gown is new or particularly handsome a boy comes deliberately out and places a lantern directly in front of the doll so that no elegant detail shall be overlooked by the audience. The puppets are, necessarily, very costly and they represent altogether quite a large amount of capital for which the theatres are often specially taxed.

The stages are quite large. The puppets are fastened by means of rods to their stands (all but the spirits and magic figures, which are worked with wires from above and float through the air). The most curious feature in the Japanese show is the manner of manipulating. The operators work on the stage in full view of the audience with the puppets placed in front of them. They speak no word and are frequently assisted by similarly mute scholars. These, to make themselves less conspicuous, often wear black-hooded robes; but the expert and favorite manipulators themselves are generally very gayly attired and their entrances are not infrequently greeted with applause. Often there are more persons working the puppets than there are puppets to be seen on the stage.

The words of the drama are read by the *Gidayu* or chanter, arrayed in a splendid ceremonial costume and sitting respectfully on a platform to the left of the stage behind a low stand upon which there rests a copy of the text. He chants loudly and musically, varying according to the nature of the account and of the characters. The chanters are artists of high standing, in fact somewhere in the seventeenth century they had already established a unique form of elocution. The reading is generally accompanied by the strains of the samisen, a three-stringed instrument, played by an artist who sits on the platform next to the chanter. Sometimes besides the principal Gidayu there are others who chant as a sort of chorus. In some performances there are as many as thirty-three Gidayus, twenty-nine samisen players, some forty manipulators and several cleaners of lamps and stage hands. The chanter, after an exciting passage, may take a sip of tea or expectorate into a little

MARIONETTES 47

bamboo cuspidor, the musicians may emphasize important lines by warning notes, the operators may jog about; Japanese audiences are accustomed to these incidental happenings and accept them with undisturbed equanimity. To Occidental witnesses they are likely to seem distractions.

There are several types of classic drama in Japan, one of which is the *Joruri*, or epical play originally composed expressly for the marionette stage. The name is derived from a drama written by a clever and beautiful court lady of Yeddo (1607-1688). It was called *The Story of The Lady Joruri* and being tremendously popular was followed by many similar plays. It was later set to samisen music and during the Eiroken period a woman singer gave performances of Joruri with puppets in Kyoto. She was so successful that she was commanded to play before noble families, finally even before the Emperor himself.

In these epic dramas there are long, poetic passages as well as narrative parts. Early in the seventeenth century Takemoto Gidayu, noted samisen player and puppet showman, invented a more brilliant presentation of puppet shows to the accompaniment of Joruri recitation and samisen music. His shows were popular with the nobility, the populace and the Samurai (who enjoyed the warlike elements in them) and he, too, was summoned to perform at the palace of the Emperor. In 1685 he established a stationary marionette theatre in Osaka called Takemoto Za. For this theatre some of Japan's best classic dramas were written. One playwright, Chikamatsu Monzayemon, the Shakespeare of Japan, together with his pupils, wrote about one hundred pieces for these puppets. In 1703 a rival theatre was founded in Osaka by a pupil of Gidayu. It was called Toyotake Za and it also had its able dramatists and enthusiastic following. The two theatres were at their zenith early in the eighteenth century; Izuma and Sosuki wrote for them. A few of their plays were in a realistic vein, such as, *The Woman's Harakari at Long Street*, or more frequently they were of a heroic temper, *The Battle of Kokusenya*, or *The Loyalty of the Five Heroes*, *The Revenge of the Soga Brothers*, and often they were such romantic affairs as the hopeless passion of two young lovers with the familiar ending of their double suicide called *shinju*.

Later in the eighteenth century the centre for puppet performances was transferred to Yeddo and flourished there for half a century in two large theatres called Hizen Za and Take Za. There were two smaller theatres, also in Kyoto. At present puppet plays are occasionally given in Tokyo at Asakusa Park. There are two such theatres also in Osaka with clever chanters and skilful puppeteers which are among the greatest attractions of the city. In the land of the cherry blossom, however, as elsewhere in this modern world, the cinema has, for a while at least, outrivaled the ancient puppet play in the affection of the people and, according to Osataro Miyamori, deprived them of a great part of their audiences.

JAPANESE PRINT (Hokusai)
Representing the famous actor, Mizuki Tatsunosuke, manipulating a puppet on a go board

MARIONETTES

But who shall belittle the remarkable achievements of the Japanese marionette theatre? All in all there have been as many as two hundred epic poets writing for the puppets and over a thousand dramas have been composed for them. Moreover, in feudal Japan, where higher education was confined to the priests and to the Samurai, the Gidayu chanters were important educators of the masses who derived their conceptions of patriotism, loyalty and ethics from the impeccable sentiments of the heroic epic dramas.

Puppets of Italy and Southern Europe

"Into whatever country we follow the footprints of the numerous, motley family of puppets, we find that however exotic their habits may be on their first arrival in the land they speedily become reflexes of the peculiar genius, tastes and characteristics of its people. Thus in Italy, the land of song and dance, of strict theatrical censorships and of despotic governments, we find the burattini dealing in sharp but polished jests at the expense of the rulers, excelling in the ballet and performing Rossini's operas without curtailment or suppression, with an orchestra of five or six instruments and singers behind the scenes. The Spanish titere couches his lance and rides forth to meet the Moor and rescue captive maidens, marches with Cortez to the conquest of Montezuma's capital or enacts with more or less decorum moving incidents from Holy Writ. In the jokken and puppen of Germany one recognizes the metaphysical and fantastical tendencies of that country, its quaint superstitions, domestic sprites and enchanted bullets. And in France, where puppet shows were early cherished and encouraged by the aristocracy as well as by the people, we need not wonder to find them elegant, witty and frivolous, modelling themselves upon their patrons."

Eclectic Magazine (1854).

EVERY country of Europe has had marionettes of one type or another persisting from very early stages through centuries of national vicissitudes. Italy, however, may be considered the pioneer, the forerunner

MARIONETTES

of them all. It was wandering Italian showmen who carried their *castelli dei burattini* into England, Germany, Spain and France, and these countries seem to have adopted puppet conventions, devices and dialogues long established by the Italians, gradually adapting them to their own tastes. The Italians have always displayed great ingenuity and perseverance in developing and elaborating their marionettes; indeed, this may be both cause and result of the perpetual joy they appear to derive from them.

There are numerous records in early Italian history of religious images in the cathedrals and monasteries, marvellous Crucifixes, figures of the Madonna and of the saints that could turn their eyes, nod their heads or move their limbs. These were the solemn forebears of the Italian fantoccini! Moreover very early it became customary for special occasions to set up elaborate stages in the naves and chapels of the churches upon which were enacted episodes from the Bible or from the lives of the martyrs. The performers were large or small figures carved and painted with rare skill and devotion, sometimes elaborately dressed and bejeweled and frequently moved by complicated mechanism. It was not unusual, in the presentation of sacred plays, to utilize both puppets and human actors together.

Vasari in his Life of *Il Cecca* tells us that, "Among others, four most solemn public spectacles took place almost every year, one for each quarter of the city with the exception of S. Giovanni for the festival of which a most solemn procession was held, as will be told. S. Maria Novella kept the feast of Ignazio, S. Croce that of S. Bartholomew called S. Baccio, S. Spirito that of the Holy Spirit and the Carmine those of the Ascension of Our Lord and the Assumption of Our Lady." Of the latter he continues, "The festival of the Ascension, then, in the church of the Carmine, was certainly most beautiful, seeing that Christ was raised from the mount, which was very well contrived in woodwork, on a cloud about and amidst which were innumerable angels, and was borne upwards into a Heaven so admirably constructed as to be really marvellous, leaving the Apostles on the mount." We may read in great detail of the impressive *Paradiso*, an arrangement of vast wheels moving in ten circles to represent the ten Heavens. These circles glittered with innumerable lights arranged in small suspended lamps which represented stars. From this Heaven or Paradiso there proceeded by means of two strong ropes, pulleys and counterweights of lead, a platform which held two angels bound firmly by the girdle to iron stakes. These in due time descend to the rood-screen and announce to the Savior that He is to ascend into Heaven. "The whole apparatus," continues the historian, "was covered with a large quantity of well-prepared wool and this gave the appearance of clouds amidst which were seen numberless cherubim, seraphim and other angels clothed in various colors." The machines and inventions were said to have been

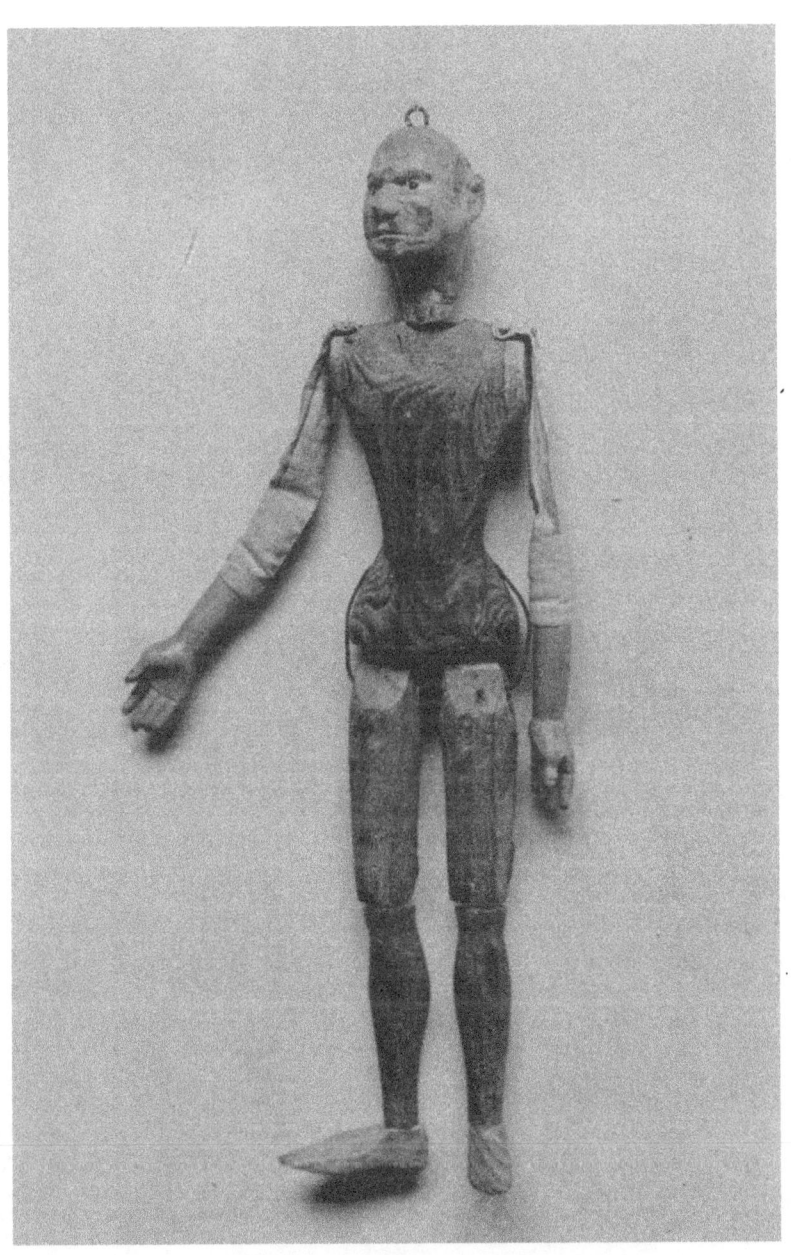

A Wooden Italian Puppet, quite old
[Property of Mr. Tony Sarg]

MARIONETTES 53

Cecca's, although Filippo Brunelleschi had made similar things long before.

"It has been pointed out," writes E. K. Chambers in the second volume of his *Mediaeval Drama*, "that the use of puppets to provide a figured representation of the mystery of the nativity seems to have preceded the use for the same purpose of living and speaking persons; and furthermore that the puppet show in the form of the Christmas Crib has outlived the drama founded upon it and is still in use in all Catholic countries." Ferrigni describes a cathedral near Naples where this ancient custom is still continued, the church being quite transformed for the occasion, its walls hidden by scenery and an imitation hill constructed at the top of which stood the Presepio. Moving figures travelled up the hill toward the manger of Bethlehem, which was illumined by a great light. I have heard such spectacles described by travelers with much enthusiasm and not a little awe. Imagine the deep impression, the reverent delight, produced among the devout worshippers in mediaeval times!

It must be admitted that many prelates condemned the use of these religious fantoccini as smacking sinfully of idolatry. Abbot Hughes of Cluny denounced them in 1086, Pope Innocent in 1210 and others also, from time to time. But canons were never able to quite eradicate the cherished custom, and the little figures always reappeared inside the churches and in adjacent cloisters and cemeteries for spectacles, mysteries and masks. The decree of the Council of Trent, however, was instrumental in forcing most of them out of the churches, so that in the sixteenth century they were generally to be found roaming about the countryside and giving performances in the marketplaces and at fairs.

There are many types of Italian pupazzi. They have been called by many names and exhibited in many manners. They are designed and dressed and manipulated in innumerable ways. In a twelfth-century manuscript discovered in the Strasbourg library there is an illustration of very primitive little *figurini*. They represent a pair of warriors caused to fight by means of two cords; the action is horizontal. Somewhat the same principle is employed to operate simple little dolls dancing on a board, generally a couple of them together, the string tied to the knee of the puppeteer. He makes the figures perform by moving his leg and generally plays on a drum or tambourine to accompany the motion. As a rule the name burattini is applied to the dolls with heads and hands fashioned of wood or paper-maché and manipulated by a hand thrust under the empty dress, a finger and a thumb fitted into the two sleeves to work the arms, another finger used to turn or bow the head of the doll. These pupazzi were most frequently played in pairs by travelling showmen with little portable castelli. Fantoccini are the puppets fashioned more or less after the human figure. They are made of cardboard or wood and occasionally

MEDIAEVAL MARIONETTES
[From an illustration in a twelfth-century manuscript in the Strassbourg library]

in part of metal or plaster. They are sometimes crudely carved, sometimes modelled with attention to every detail. They are operated by means of wires or threads connecting them with the control, which is in the hands of the marionettist standing concealed above. The number and arrangement of threads and controls may be simple or intricate. Sometimes the limbs are wired and all the wires except those of the arms are carried out of the head through an iron tube. Another device is that of wiring the dolls and manipulating them from below by pedals. There is no end to the variety of contrivances invented by the makers of marionettes. The more elaborate dolls are generally exhibited in large and substantial castelli or on permanent stages constructed in private homes or in theatres used entirely for fantocinni, the spectacular effects being carried out on an amazing scale.[1]

From earliest times the marionettes have been

[1] There are many Italian names for the puppets. From *pupa*, meaning doll, is derived *pupazzi*. From *fantoccia*, also signifying doll, we have *fantoccini*, or little dolls. From *figura*, statue or figure, comes *figurini*, statuettes or little figures. *Burattini* comes from *buratto*, cloth, being made mostly of cloth. *Marionette* is a modification of *Maria*, the Virgin, meaning little Maries from the early statuettes in churches. Another explanation is found in the tenth century Venetian *Festival of the Maries*. Upon one occasion Barbary pirates carried off twelve Venetian maidens in their bridal procession. The rape of the affianced Virgins was avenged by Venetian youths and thereafter celebrated annually by a procession of richly dressed girls. These later were replaced by elaborately gowned figures carried year by year in the procession — hence Marionetti, little Maries.

exceedingly popular with both learned and ignorant. Every village was visited by ambulant shows, every city had its large castello, frequently many of them, while noble families had their private puppet theatres and engaged distinguished writers to compose plays. Lorenzo de Medici is said to have enjoyed puppet shows and to have given many of them. Cosimo I is reported to have had the fantoccini in the Palazzo Vecchio, Francesco I in the Uffizi: Girolamo Cardan, celebrated mathematician and physician wrote in 1550, "An entire day would not be sufficient in which to describe these puppets that play, fight, shoot, dance and make music." Leone Allaci, librarian of the Vatican under Pope Alexander VII, stopped nightly to watch the burattini play. Prominent mechanicians and scientists used their skill to create clever *pupazzi*; artists have left us charming pictures of groups thronging around the castelli in the public roads; poets and scholars wrote plays for the marionettes.

In the beginning the repertory of the pupazzi was derived entirely from the *sacre rappresentazione*, consisting of scenes from the Old and the New Testaments, stories of miracles and martyrdoms. Soon a comic element was allowed to creep in, the better to hold the attention of the audience. Fables were introduced for variety, and episodes from heroic tales of chivalry, also satires reminiscent of Roman decadence. The latter were performed by puppets fantastically dressed and burlesqueing local types,

FIGURES USED FOR CHRISTMAS CRIB INSIDE THE CHURCH
Seventeenth or eighteenth century
[From the collection of Mr. Sumner Healey, New York]

MARIONETTES

and, naturally, speaking in the native dialect of those particular characters. The showman improvised the dialogue to fit the occasion, using only a skeleton plot to direct the action just as did the actors of the *Commedia dell'Arte*. "Thus," claims an authority on Italian puppetry, "on this humble stage were born types of the ancient Italian theatre, the immortal masks." It might be as difficult to prove as to disprove this statement, but at any rate the pupazzi had a hand in popularizing and perpetuating the famous *maschere*.

At this point it might be well to digress for a moment and to consider the commedia dell'arte which is so interwoven with the story of Italian marionettes. Along with the commedia erudita which was flourishing at the courts of the great Italian princes there developed an extemporaneous, popular theatre depending greatly for its spirit upon the invention and talent of the actors. Perhaps the beginnings of its gay humor may be traced back to the comic and local elements introduced into the early *sacre rappresentazione*. Perhaps the characters were copied from the familiar buffoons of Latin comedy. At any rate, the well-known masks or *personaggi* of the cast represented amusing types from all strata of Italian society, and each was immediately recognizable by a conventionalized and rather grotesque costume. *Arlecchino*, who originally came from Bergamo, is the chief personage of this motley group. He is a unique figure in his strange suit of multi-colored patches, his black mask, his peculiar weapon, all reminiscent of the Roman *Histrio*. At first conceived as a happy, simple fellow, he became in time a character of unbridled gayety and pointed wit. Then there was *Pulcinella*, descended probably from the Roman *Maccus*, a Neapolitan rogue and merry-maker whose white costume serves to accentuate the hump in his back and his other physical peculiarities. There were *Scaramuccia*, also of Naples, false bravo and coward, *Stentorella*, from Florence, a mean miserly wretch, *Cassandrino*, the charming fop and braggart, a Roman invention. *Messer Pantalone* is a good-natured Venetian merchant deceived by all, *Scapino* is the mischief maker apt to lead youth astray, *Constantine* of Verona is "said youth." Then come *Brighella, Capitaine, Pierrot*, world renowned, *Columbine, Isabella*, and a host of other Italian conceptions, to say nothing of *Pasquino, Peppinno, Ornofrio* and *Rosina* who are the masks of Sicily.

It was customary to have the plot and the principal situations sketchily outlined for the actors. They then went into the play supplying dialogue and improvising action and appropriate jests as the mood of the moment dictated. The humor of the theatre was merry and spontaneous, though frequently extremely broad and of questionable taste. But despite this license of manners, the morals and purposes of the plays were good, levelling shafts of satire against the frauds and abuses of the age, poking fun and scorn at rogueries, hypocrisies, weaknesses.

PULCINELLA IN ITALY
[From original color lithograph]

MARIONETTES

The commedia dell'arte flourished brilliantly for a century or more. Flaminio Scala was the first director who attempted to systematize it. In 1611 he published a number of scenarii and detailed directions for the action. However, in time the unbridled wit degenerated into mere vulgarity, the grace and spontaneity of gesture into absurd acrobatic tricks and grimacing, the bubbling jests and startling situations became stale. It was then that Goldoni came to reform the Italian drama. In his plays, it is true, one may still find traces of the popular masks, but they are relegated to minor rôles, subdued and propperly clad. They will never wholly die out.

Through various stages of the Italian drama the marionettes have trailed gayly along, ever adopting the new without discarding the old. Their repertoire is all inclusive. They have enacted sacred dramas and legends of saints, *Sansone e Dalila*, *Sante Tecla*, *Guida Iscaretta* and innumerable others. They have made use of the scenarios of old Latin plays such as *Amor non virtoso* and *Il Basilico di Berganasso*. When the bombastic, elaborate plays were discarded by the actors they came into possession of the puppet showmen. Thereafter the burattini became grandiloquent, and stalked about as princes and heroes of tragedy, while their trappings and settings often grew correspondingly elaborate. To fables of heroes and pastoral scenes, to the romances of Paladins and Saracens and spectacular tales of brigands, assassins and tyrants were added the pathetic and romantic melodramas of foreign lands. *Il Flauto magico, La donna Serpente, Genovieffa di Brabante, Elizabetta Potowsky,* everything was to be seen in the castelli of the fantoccini, even the military plays of Iffland and Kotzebue. Moreover Arlecchino and his band were always allowed to enter at any time, into any situation. Indeed, when the commedia dell'arte became at last discredited on the larger stage it sought shelter with the puppets. Thus in the puppet booths the popular old personaggi were kept alive among the people, where they had, indeed, been ever very much at home.

These old masks continue to be found to-day in the puppet shows of Italy, as are also the melodramatic tragedies popular with the masses and the clever, satirical comedies given in more intellectual circles. Stendhal (Marie Henri Beyle), in his *Voyage en Italie,* reports that in Rome he witnessed a wonderful performance of Machiavelli's *Mandragore* performed for a select and highly cultured circle by marvellous little marionettes on a stage scarcely five feet wide but perfect in every detail. Rome has always abounded in puppet theatres. Ernest Peixotto writes in 1903 that noblemen were in the habit of giving plays acted by fantoccini in their palaces, plays reeking with escapades and political satire that dared not show its face on the public boards. Stendhal wrote also that he found Cassandrino at the *Teatro Fiano* very much the vogue, presented as a fashionable man of the world falling in love with every petticoat. Teoli, who had made the part famous, was an engraver by profession as well as an expert marionettist. His delightful little Cassandrino was sometimes allowed to appear in a three-cornered hat and scarlet coat suggesting the cardinal, sometimes as a foppish Roman citizen, clever and experienced but still with a weakness for the ladies. He was a charming instrument for voicing popular criticism against the ecclesiastics and the government. What wonder that Teoli's theatre was sometimes closed and he himself imprisoned? But Gregory XVI reopened the theatre and long after Teoli's death it remained in the hands of his family.

At the present time in what was formerly this very Fiano theatre, in the Piazza S. Apollinare, there still exists a prominent show of fantoccini. Here the small auditorium is perfectly fitted out for the accommodation of the very respectable middle-class audience with a sprinkling of the aristocracy. The stage is well lighted, there is an orchestra, the dolls are beautifully, nay, elegantly dressed. Here we find Pulcinella entering into the plays, a well-mannered, dexterous Pulcinella. The ballet is amazingly graceful, often ending with a tableau or even fireworks.

The most popular puppet theatre in Rome to-day, however, seems to be that in the Piazza Montanara. Here the rather primitive fantoccini present, most frequently, the ancient tales of chivalry from Ariosto but their repertory also includes such diverse dramatic material as *Aeneas, King of Tunis* and *The Dis-*

covery of the Indies by Christopher Columbus. The audience sitting in the pit is composed chiefly of rough, bronzed working men with thick, unkempt hair, a noisy crowd all eating cakes or cracking pumpkin seeds between their teeth. A spectator thus describes a performance: "To-day they are to perform the lovely tale of *Angellica and Medoro,* or *Orlando Furioso and the Paladins.* The curtain rises and the marionettes appear. The valiant Roland and Pulcinella, his squire, come forth with a bound and neither of them touches the ground. Roland is covered with iron from head to foot and holds in his hand the Durlindana, [his sword]. Pulcinella has white stockings, a white costume, with wide sleeves, and a white cap with a tassel. The marionettes are two feet high, their limbs perfectly supple, and lend themselves to any movement, etc. etc."

The same account tells us that the play of *Christopher Columbus* had been given here fourteen evenings in succession, three times an evening. In it the Indians excited special curiosity, decked out with splendid plumes.

In 1912 Mr. W. Story visited a similar theatre of fantoccini in Genoa where elaborate productions (usually of the wars of the Paladins) were presented to an ever-receptive audience. "What is that great noise of drums inside?" inquired Mr. Story of the ticket seller. "Battaglio," was the reproving reply, "E sempre battaglie!" (Always battle!) Although this perpetual fray was rather crude, it was followed

ITALIAN PUPPET BALLET
[From a drawing in Hermann S. Rehm's *Das Buch der Marionetten*]

by an excellent ballet which danced the most intricate steps with masterly ease and grace.

There is an account by Charles Dickens of the show which he witnessed in Genoa. It is too entertaining to be omitted.

"The Theatre of Puppets, or *Marionetti*, a famous company from Milano, is, without any exception, the drollest exhibition I ever beheld in my life, etc.

"The comic man in the comedy I saw one summer night, is a waiter at a hotel. There never was such a locomotive actor since the world began. Great pains are taken with him. He has extra joints in his legs, and a practical eye, with which he winks at the pit, in a manner that is absolutely insupportable to a stranger, but which the initiated audience, mainly composed of the common people, receive (as they do everything else) quite as a matter of course, and as if he were a man. His spirits are prodigious. He continually shakes his legs, and winks his eye.

"There is a heavy father with grey hair, who sits down on the regular conventional stage-bank, and blesses his daughter in the regular conventional way, who is tremendous. No one would suppose it possible that anything short of a real man could be so tedious. It is the triumph of art.

"In the ballet, an Enchanter runs away with the Bride, in the very hour of her nuptials. He brings her to his cave, and tries to soothe her. They sit down on a sofa (the regular sofa! in the regular place, O. P. Second Entrance!) and a procession of musicians enter; one creature playing a drum, and knocking himself off his legs at every blow. These failing to delight her, dancers appear. Four first; then two; the two; the flesh-coloured two. The way in which they dance; the height to which they spring; the impossible and inhuman extent to which they pirouette; the revelation of their preposterous legs; the coming down with a pause, on the very tips of their toes, when the music requires it; the gentleman's retiring up, when it is the lady's turn; and the lady's retiring up when it is the gentleman's turn; the final passion of a pas-de-deux; and going off with a bound! I shall never see a real ballet, with a composed countenance, again.

"I went, another night, to see these Puppets act a play called 'St. Helena, or the Death of Napoleon.' It began by the disclosure of Napoleon, with an immense head, seated on a sofa in his chamber at St. Helena; to whom his valet entered, with this obscure announcement:

"'Sir Yew ud se on Low!' (The ow, as in cow).

"Sir Hudson (that you could have seen his regimentals!) was a perfect mammoth of a man, to Napoleon; hideously ugly; with a monstrously disproportionate face, and a great clump for the lower-jaw, to express his tyrannical and obdurate nature.

"He began his system of persecution by calling his prisoner 'General Buonaparte'; to which the latter replied, with the deepest tragedy, 'Sir Yew ud se on Low, call me not thus. Repeat that phrase and leave me! I am Napoleon, Emperor of France!' Sir Yew ud se on, nothing daunted, proceeded to entertain him with an ordinance of the British Government, regulating the state he should preserve, and the furniture of his rooms; and limiting his attendants to four or five persons. 'Four or five for me!' said Napoleon. 'Me! One hundred thousand men were lately at my sole command; and this English officer talks of four or five for me!'

"Throughout the piece, Napoleon (who talked very like the real Napoleon, and was forever having small soliloquies by himself) was very bitter on 'these English soldiers' to the great satisfaction of the audience, who were perfectly delighted to have Low bullied; and who, whenever Low said 'General Buonaparte' (which he always did; always receiving the same correction) quite execrated him. It would be hard to say why; for Italians have little cause to sympathize with Napoleon, Heaven knows.

"There was no plot at all, except that a French officer, disguised as an Englishman, came to propound a plan of escape, and being discovered (but not before Napoleon had magnanimously refused to steal his freedom), was immediately ordered off by Low to be hanged, in two very long speeches, which Low made memorable, by winding up with 'Yas!' to show that he was English, which brought down thunders of applause. Napoleon was so affected by this catastrophe, that he fainted away on the spot, and was carried out by two other puppets.

"Judging from what followed, it would appear that he never recovered from the shock; for the next act showed him, in a clean shirt, in his bed (curtains crimson and white), where a lady, prematurely dressed in mourning, brought two little children, who kneeled down by the bedside, while he made a decent end; the last word on his lips being 'Vatterlo.'

"Dr. Antommarchi was represented by a puppet with long lank hair, like Mawworm's, who, in consequence of some derangement of his wires, hovered about the couch like a vulture, and gave medical opinions in the air. He was almost as good as Low, though the latter was great at all times, a decided brute and villain, beyond all possibility of mistake. Low was especially fine at the last, when, hearing the doctor and the valet say, 'The Emperor is dead!' he pulled out his watch, and wound up the piece (not the watch) by exclaiming, with characteristic brutality, 'Ha! ha! Eleven minutes to six! The General dead! and the spy hanged!'

"This brought the curtain down, triumphantly."

Goethe was greatly interested by the shows in Naples where every event of local interest was introduced upon the puppet stage. The humor of the Neapolitan Pulcinella was often vulgar; ladies were not supposed to visit the shows, although they were frequently given in fine society. On the street where they were most popular, however, they drew about them picturesque audiences reminiscent of Hogarth's

MARIONETTES

sketches. Pulcinella was made to speak with a squeaky voice by means of the pivetta, a little metal contrivance placed in the mouth of the actor. It is formed of two curved pieces of tin or brass, bound together and hollow inside. The voice, passing through this, acquired a shrill and ridiculous sound.

Until the eighteenth century the puppets enjoyed celebrity and prestige in Venice. Vittorio Malmani tells us that from the sixteenth century when they became the vogue among Italian nobility, Venetian patricians were accustomed to build elaborate little puppet theatres in their palaces. One example of this was that of Antonio Labia, who exactly reproduced in miniature the huge theatre, S. Giovanni Grisostomo, famous throughout Europe, stage, boxes, decorations, machinery, lighting facilities, costumes — everything precisely imitated the larger theatre. The actors were figurines of wax and wood. The first drama produced here was *Lo Starnuto d'Ercole* (The Sneeze of Hercules) which we may find described in Goldini's memoirs.

In the Piazza of San Marco and in the Piazzetta until the fall of the Republic, so Malamani tells us, the castelli of the burattini were numerous during carnival time. In the eighteenth century the *casotti* of Paglialunga and Bordogna were great rival attractions until the former showman died and his little actors went to swell the company of Bordogna, whose descendants continued the theatre throughout the eighteenth century. The casotto of Bordogna has been painted by the brush of Longhi, standing near the great dove of the Ducal Palace.

A. Calthrop tells of his recent visit to a rough little place, *Teatro Minerva*, where three-foot burattini, looking life size, were manipulated crudely to the intense satisfaction of the audience. He mentions a well-managed maschere, Guillette and her lover, a clownish dwarf, both speaking in the Venetian dialect, and after the play, the marionette ballet. Another account tells of a pretty little puppet theatre with boxes, galleries and parquet where dolls thirty-five inches high play classic tragedy of four or five acts and comedy and pantomime, including always a marvellous ballet. Here the most admired puppet receives encores, even bouquets and very properly bows in response. The stages of such little theatres are as complete as the most luxurious real stages. The figures can sit on chairs, open bureau drawers, carry objects, and they are carefully and beautifully costumed. The dialogue and subjects are far removed from the triviality of the crude castelli, where the pupazzi are manipulated on the fingers of the showman. It is not unusual to witness *Nebuccodnoser* performed by fantoccini or Rossini's operas.

In recent issues of *The Marionette* one will find an enthusiastic eulogy of a remarkable puppet theatre in Torino, the proprietors of which were the Lupi brothers. They had inherited their profession from their grandfather, a wandering showman of Ferrara,

MARIONETTES

and from their father, a man of lively talent who had established the present theatre. The two brothers were named Luigi I and Luigi II, respectively; only one is still living. Their show has been taken far and wide. It travelled from Buenos Aires to London, from Chicago to Venice, and has gained as great applause as did the puppets of the famous Prandi brothers of Brescia in their day. The repertory embraces the universe in time and space, extends from the flood to the siege of Makalle; comprises mythology, natural history and city news; stretches from China to California, from Cafrena to Greenland, from spaces in the air to abysses of ocean, from the circles of Paradise to the caverns of Hell. It includes the old commedia dell'arte, dramas from all literatures, the ballets of Pratesi and Manzotti, the operas of Meyerbeer and Verdi, all the military glories of the nation from the battle of Goito to the occupation of Rome, all the congresses, earthquakes, epidemics, floods, coronations, exhibitions, etc.

In Bologna flourished the show founded by Filippo Cuccoli, whose clever invention of the character Sandrone became so popular. In the hands of the son, Angelo Cuccoli, the puppets continued until 1905, delighting the public with their sprightly gayety.

In Bologna, too, lived the marionettist whom Gordon Craig designates simply but reverently as *Maestro*. His trade was that of a watchmaker, but he was a master showman of burattini, and the shows in his unpretentious castello are the true evidences of his devotion and deep understanding of the art of the marionette.

There are, it is claimed, over four hundred edifizi for marionettes, large and small, in Italy, to say nothing of the wandering booths of which there are two or three times as many. The large mechanical theatres compete with regular players.

The most modern maschere on the puppet stage has changed a little in appearance, if not in spirit from the ancient masks. We are told of a miniature Tartaglia, who twists his lips into a grimace; of a puppet, Rogantino, who grinds his teeth; of Stenterello, who can put his finger to his nose and scratch it; and of the newer mask, Carciofo, who has a hollow metallic case for a body which enables him to eat macaroni, drink and smoke. He can also undress himself! In North Italy, Gian Duja is a puppet hero whose exploits delight the public almost as much as those of the Paladins. He is of Piedmontese origin. He slays whomever he encounters, modern politics being mixed up with his various and mighty adventures.

The marionettes are an absorbing interest for the people of Sicily. There is something appealing about the audiences of the usual modest theatrino. It is composed entirely of men and boys; many of them may have eaten dry bread without cheese or onions to save the small sum required for admission. The people of the country are very poor, but this is their

MARIONETTES

favorite diversion. So they sit crowded into a dark little hall, spellbound for hours, transported into a world of romance which their spirits crave. It may be filled with crude, primitive puppets, but it is glorified by the vivid intensity of their imaginations.

The Sicilian shows are not very unlike the Italian. One finds farces with local maschere, grotesque comedy, passion-plays, tragedies and occasional ballets. But of all plays those forever and most intensely adored are the ones founded upon the episodes of Ariosto's *Orlando Furioso*. Night after night the successions of thrilling adventures proceed. Year after year the same dramas are presented, regardless of historic veracity or of the artistic unities; their spell remains the same. Time cannot wither nor custom stale their infinite invariability. The spectators recognize (nay, they anticipate) each puppet hero or villain as he enters. They know every detail of every character's costume. They have the order of events by heart.

Mr. Henry Festing Jones, wandering delightfully in Sicily, visited a show in Trapani where the burattini were presenting some version of the Paladins of France. Before entering, his guide, Pasquale, informed him: "She will die to-night." He referred to Bradamante. Mr. Jones expressed regret and asked for particulars, whereupon Pasquale elucidated: "She will die of grief at the loss of her husband." And so, indeed, she did. It proved an affecting scene and was read with deep pathos. The

Empress Marfisa, searching for Bradamante in the woods, finds her prostrate in a grotto. "Farewell, sister, I am dying." Then she dies. An angel flutters down and receives her soul from her lips.

More thrilling, of course, was the fighting of the red-eyed Ferrain, performed the same night (red-eyed, incidentally, "because he was always in a rage"). The first episode presented Ferrain and Angelica whose husband he killed. "He cut off Duca d'Anela's head, which rolled about on the stage. Immediately there came three Turks. Ferrain stabbed each as he entered, one, two, three, and their bodies encumbered the ground as the curtain fell.

"It rose as soon as the bodies had been removed, Ferrain stamping about alone. There came three more Turks. He stabbed them as they came, one, two, three, and their bodies encumbered the ground. To them there came three knights in armour; Ferrain fought them all three together for a very considerable time and it was deafening. He killed them all. Their bodies, etc., together with those of the three Turks. A bloody sight."

These fantoccini of Trapani were large and crude, dressed in heavy armor. An iron rod, extending up from the head, another attached to the sword hand served for the moving and manipulating of them. Strings were employed to raise the vizier, etc. The legs and arms were apt to swing rather wildly in the heat of the fray, the combatants often sweeping off their feet through the air. Then armor clashed

MARIONETTES

against armor, body against body, swords shivering against shield. Truly, an amazing display!

However naïve or even childishly absurd some of these exaggerated episodes may appear, viewed with a sympathetic eye they become manifestations of unconscious romance in the spirit of the Sicilian people, a curiously mingled heritage which is theirs. While the Paladins and Saracens heroically stamp across the boards of the puppet show, one may sit back and recall the many great races dwelling about the Mediterranean, which have had their influence in Sicily from the Phoenicians and Greeks, Normans and Saracens down. One remembers the reign of the Emperor Frederick II, the strange blending of East and West, the Christian cathedrals of Moslem design and decoration, a time inspired by the songs of the troubadours wandering through the blossoming land and spreading their spell of Carolingian chivalry and romance.

The familiarity of the people with the long and intricate legends they love so well is humorously portrayed by Mr. Henry Festing Jones. This author was particularly fortunate in having formed a friendship with a very busy *buffo* of Palermo and with his entire family. Hence the illuminating intimacy of his visits behind the scenes. In a letter anticipating Mr. Jones' visit, the buffo writes concerning his show that the marionettes had just produced *Samson* and that, "just now in *The Story of the Paladine*, Orlando is throwing away his arms and running about naked in the woods, mad for the love of Angelica, and soon we shall have the burning of Bizerta and the destruction of the Africans. This will finish in July and then we shall begin *The Story of Guido Santo.*" This programme appears to have been carried out in order, for Mr. Jones, arriving at the *teatrino*, found the performance of *Guido Santo* in full swing.

"The buffo," he writes, "took me into his workshop to show me two inflammable Turkish pavilions which he was making. Ettorina in her madness was to fire them in a few days, one in the afternoon, the other at the evening repetition, as a conclusion to the spectacle. I inquired, 'Who was Ettorina and why did she go mad?' It appeared, at great length, that she went mad for love of Ruggiero Persiano.

"Next morning," continues the narrator, "I called on the buffo in his workshop. The two inflammable Turkish pavilions were finished, ready to be fired by Ettorina, and he was full of his devils." This led to another question: "I never heard of Argantino before. Did you say he was the son of Malagigi?"

"That is right. He did not happen to be at Roncesvalles, so he was not killed with Orlando and the other paladins. An angel came to him and said, 'Now the Turks will make much war against the Chrstians and, since the Christians always want a magician, it is the will of Heaven that you shall have the rod of Malagigi, who is no longer here, and that Guido Santo shall have la Durlindana, the sword of Orlando.' And it was so, and Argantino thereafter appeared as a pilgrim."

"I remember about Malagigi; he made all of Rinaldo's armor."

"Excuse me, he made some of his armor; but he did not make his helmet, nor his sword Fusberta, nor his horse Baiardo. First you must know that Rinaldo was one of the four brothers, sons of Amone, and their sister was Bradamante."

"I saw her die at Trapani. The Empress Marfisa came and found her dying of grief in a grotto for loss of her husband, Ruggiero da Risa."

"Precisely; she was Marfisa's sister-in-law because she married Marfisa's brother, Ruggiero da Risa."

"Then who was the cavaliere errante, Ruggiero Persiano?"

"He was the son of Marfisa and Guidon Selvaggio, and this Guidon Selvaggio was the son of Rinaldo."

"Had Bradamante no children?"

"Guido Sante is the son of Bradamante and Ruggiero da Risa."

"I heard something about Guido Sante in Castellinaria the other day. Let me see, what was it? Never mind. I hope he left children."

"I told you last year that he never married."

"Oh, yes, of course; what was I thinking of? One cannot remember everything at once and pedigrees are always confusing at first. Then it was for love of Bradamante's nephew by marriage, Ruggiero Persiano, that Ettorina has now gone mad?"

"Bravo. And Malagigi was Bradamante's cousin." The buffo then continued to tell the story of Malagigi and Argantino. How Malagigi, the sorcerer, albeit a Christian, began to have fears of not getting into Heaven when he died, hence decided to repent and burn all his magic books but one. After having accomplished this, he summoned his confidential and private devil and commanded, "Convey me to some peaceful shore where I may repent of my sins and die of grief in a grotto."

Here his friend objected that this made "consecutive fifths" with his cousin Bradamante dying of grief in a grotto in Trapani. The buffo admitted it would have been better if one of them had had the originality to die in bed as a Christian, but that it was the will of Heaven and could not be altered; besides the people who missed the death of Bradamante would be pleased to see Malagigi die. After repenting like S. Gerolamo in his grotto, Malagigi died there. A long time after his son Argantino and his second cousin Guido Santo were travelling in Asia and found the tomb. Guido knelt down, saying, "I perceive here a sepulchre."

Presently the tomb opened and Malagigi's skeleton rattled up and spoke to them. He gave his magic book to Argantino, the horse Sfrenato to Guido and made them swear to preserve the faith. After his skeleton retired to the tomb it closed by a miracle while a ball of fire ran over the stage. "And all this," said the buffo, "happened only last Friday.

MARIONETTES

Why did you not come in time to see it? It was very emotional."

Later the buffo gave a private performance of this emotional scene and then "to take the taste of the skeleton out of our mouths," as Mr. Jones puts it, he brought forth a *Ballo Fantastico*. It was done by a heavy Turk who danced himself to pieces, each limb falling off and being changed into a little devil, the head into a wizard and so on, until there were sixteen different devils, wizards, serpents, etc., from the one original Turk. After this there came on a marvellous rope-dancer, extraordinarily lifelike and amusing.

At Catania, at the *Teatro Sicilia* of Gregorio Grasso, Mr. Jones saw *The Passion* performed by puppets during Holy Week. Every scene was presented in detail, from the meeting of the Sanhedrin and the conspiracy between Annas and Caiaphas to destroy the Nazarene to the Resurrection and the Ascension. The figures were all newly costumed for this occasion and their faces freshly painted, but there lingered about the soldiers a flavor reminiscent of the Paladins. The scenes were arranged quite in the manner of the paintings of old masters. The table set for the Last Supper and the puppets seated around it strongly suggested Leonardo da Vinci. The figure of Jesus, although not wholly successful, was manipulated with great understanding. It moved but little, and then with simple, slow gestures; it was allowed to speak only the few words given to Christ in the Gospels.

When it caused a miracle, a great light appeared and there was music. The puppets here also performed the *Nativita* at Christmas. For the rest they had the usual Sicilian repertory.

In Spain, as in Italy, one may trace the beginnings of puppetry back to the ecclesiastic ceremonies in churches and monasteries where articulated figures presented scenes from Holy Writ and legends of saints and martyrs, — all this notwithstanding repeated canonical prohibitions. These little figures remained as late as the sixteenth century in the churches of Seville. We are told by Charles Magnin that at the commencement of the seventeenth century a synod was held at Orhuela, a little Valencian bishopric which solemnly forbade "admission into churches of small images of the Virgin and female saints, curled, painted, covered with jewels and dressed in silks and resembling courtesans."

The emperor, Charles V, had a great love for curious and ingenious mechanical toys, and with such encouragement many mechanicians applied themselves to the invention of automatic contrivances. Giovanni Torriani is said to have won favor by constructing a very wonderful clock. When Charles V abdicated his throne and retired to the monastery of Cremona, the loyal Torriani followed him to his retreat, and many an hour this famous mathematician spent distracting the saddened monarch with marionette shows. He constructed marvellous *titeres*,

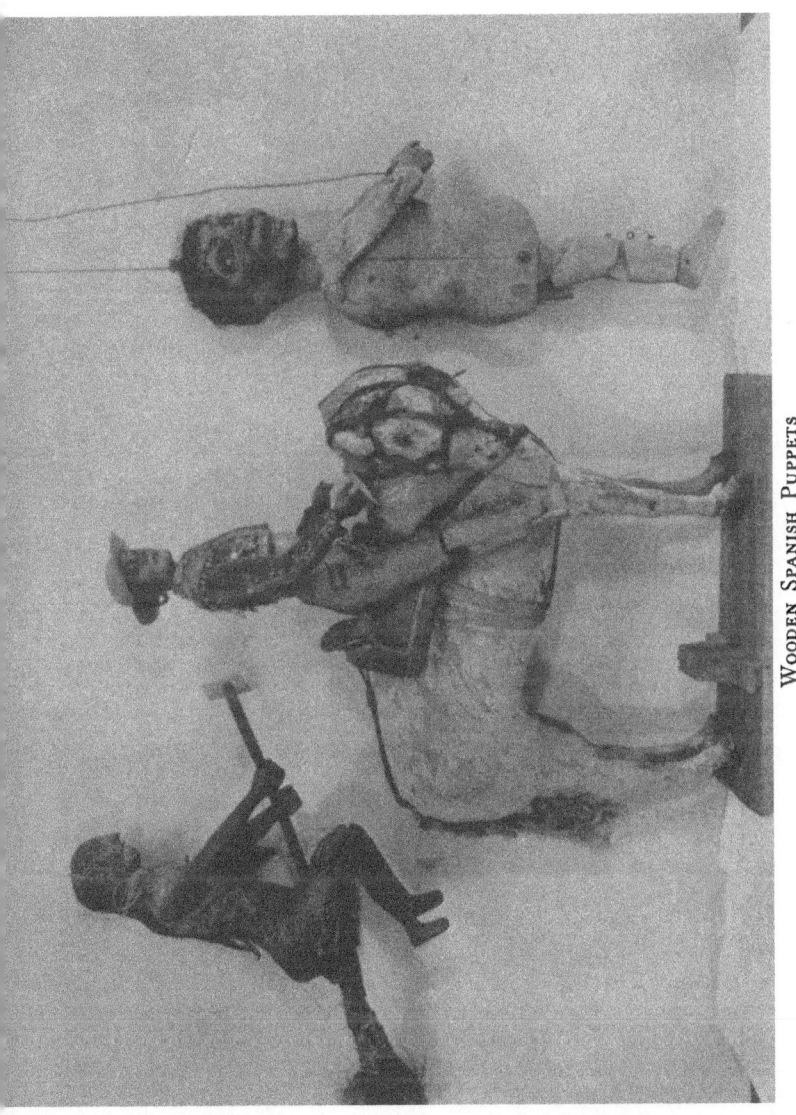

WOODEN SPANISH PUPPETS
Part of a large and elaborate set
[Courtesy of the Bradlay Studios, New York]

MARIONETTES

as the Spanish puppets are called, little armed men who blew horns, beat drums, and fought; little horses and even miniature bull-fights.

At the marriage festival of Louis XIV and the Infanta Maria Teresa a feature in the procession which welcomed Mazarin's arrival in Spain was a group of mammoth Moors and their wives, which moved ponderously along by means of very intricate internal mechanisms.

There had previously been theatrical puppets in Spain, but these mechanical improvements were soon adopted by the popular *titereros*, showmen, and the marionettes sprung up in all public places, in cities, villages, fairs, even at court.

The characters and repertories of the titeres were always strictly national, although the exhibitors were frequently foreigners. Moors, knights, giants, enchanters, conquerors of the Indies, saints, hermits, bull-fighters, characters from the old and new testaments, all were displayed in the puppet castello. The Spanish *Grazioso*, costumed somewhat in the fashion of Pierrot, was never a very prominent puppet; he later acquired the name of Don Christobal Pulichinela. A well-known type of wandering show consisted of a blind man, led by a boy, with a mule and wagon to carry the castello and equipment. The blind man generally recited the text of the play, the boy operated the puppets. Cervantes depicts a Spanish show for us where Don Quixote and Sancho Panza saw performed, "The manner in which Signor

Gayferos accomplished the deliverance of his spouse Melisandra," and he relates with much spirit how Don Quixote's chivalrous zeal interfered with the performance of Master Peter's puppets. Since that time, over three hundred years, there has been little change in the titeres of Spain.

In 1877 in Madrid Molière's *Monsieur Pourceaugnac* was presented by marionettes. In 1808 a French savant was present at a Valencian puppet show when the *Death of Seneca* was performed. The account tells us that, "In the presence of the audience the celebrated philosopher ended historically by opening his veins in a bath. The streams of blood that flowed from his arms were simulated cleverly enough by the movement of red ribbon. An unexpected miracle, less historic than the mode of his death, wound up the drama. Amidst the noise of fireworks the pagan sage was taken up into Heaven in a *glory*, pronouncing, as he ascended, the confession of his faith in Jesus Christ to the perfect-satisfaction of the audience. Spain, a country of anomalies, is not to be disconcerted by an anachronism."

In Portugal the titeres were used so frequently to represent hermits and monks in monkish garb that they come to be called *Bonifrates*. They were quite similar to the Spanish marionettes.

The Puppets in France

'Ainsi font font font
Les petites marionettes
Elles font font
Trois petits tours et puis s'en vont."

THE French, scarcely less than the Italians, are devotees of the diminutive Polichinelle. Moreover in France this devotion is particularly noticeable in the upper classes. Perhaps it is this interest of aristocratic and cultured circles or possibly the happy genius and good taste of the people themselves which have endowed the marionettes of France with such undeniable charm, a sort of chic cleverness and at times a rare and finished beauty.

The ancient Gauls, before their conquest by the Romans, had great Druid gods, Belen, Esus, Witolf, Murcia, represented by huge and fearful idols which were operated by means of internal mechanism to terrorize into submission the fierce, barbaric worshipers who beheld their solemn gestures. After the conquest Greek and Roman practices were intermingled with barbarian rites and, eventually, the doctrine of Christianity was infused into the mass of strange beliefs and superstitions. But even in the fifteenth and sixteenth centuries, after the new religion had become established in the land, its priests continued to employ the moving images as they had done in the churches of Italy. Similarly too, we find the sacred representations and religious rites within the churches giving birth to the mysteries and morality plays just outside which gradually spread to booths in the market places and roamed the countryside under the guidance of ambulant showmen. In the Provençal cribs, the *Crèches parlantes* of the southern cities at Christmas time, there are to-day many qualities remaining from these old mysteries; the large decorated stages, the technical devices, the transformations, the beautifully dressed, articulated dolls, the music and recitations.

One characteristic of the great French *mitouries* was the use, frequently and openly, of human actors along with marionettes. Many records of such performances have been preserved, among them a description of one celebrated annually at Dieppe on the first day of August by a company of clergy and laity supported by several figures set in motion by means of strings and counterweights. In the open space before the Church of St. James there was represented the *Mystery of the Assumption*. Four hundred *personaggi* participated and the marvellous spectacle attracted throngs of strangers to the city of Dieppe. Similar performances at Christmas, Easter, or at other times were given in all the larger cities of France, in Rouen, Lyons, Paris, Marseilles. The plays were of a religious character. Notable as late as the seventeenth century were the spectacles produced by the monks of the Order of Théatines with clever movable figures upon the presepio they constructed before their convent door. These monks won the favor of no less a persònage than Jules Mazarin, who had them give performances in Paris.

But, as these religious puppets ventured out from the jeweled twilight of the cathedrals into the bright sunshine they were accosted by flippant crews of wanderers from the South, Pulcinella, Arlecchino, Dottore, Cassandrino, Columbine, and other protagonists of Italian puppet drama, exploring in their castelli the highroads and villages of a new country. The merry foreigners intermingled happily with the native *fantoches;* they altered their names and their natures with easy adaptability and upon the French puppet stage appeared in sprightly guise *Polichinelle, Harlequin, Pierrot.*

French theatrical puppets must have become established in the sixteenth century for we find them mentioned in a work entitled *Serées* published 1584, by Guillaume Bouchet, juge et consul des marchands à Poitier. Polichinelle first presented himself to the Parisian public about 1630 and although not yet at the height of his glory he was completely changed into a buffoon of Gascony. In 1649 the marionettes entered into the first permanent stage erected in Paris for the *jeu des marionettes*, by the side of the Porte de Nesle. The proprietors of this theatre were two brothers (or father and son as some prefer to consider them) from Bologna, Giovanni and Francesco Briocci, the name changed by the French to Brioché. It is said that Brioché first displayed his dolls to attract clients for himself as he originally plied the trade of dentist. At any rate Francesco carved the dolls and Giovanni improvised the dialogue in French interspersed with quaint Italian or Latin sayings. So amusing were these burattini that they became tremendously the rage. We find Brioché mentioned in the works of the academician, Perrault, and in 1677 Nicolas Boileau speaks of him as a well known figure in the Parisian streets, "Là non loin de la place où Brioché préside, etc."

There is a well known story concerning Cyrano de Bergerac and a trained ape of Brioché, *Fagotin* by name. A contemporary account of the incident thus describes the animal: "He was as big as a little man and a devil of a droll. His master had put on him an old Spanish hat whose dilapidations were concealed by a plume: round his neck was a frill à la Scaramouche; he wore a doublet with six movable skirts trimmed with lace and tags, — a garment that gave him rather the look of a lackey, — and a shoulder belt from which hung a pointless blade." One day Cyrano saw the monkey arrayed in this livery wandering and grimacing about the puppet booth. But the poet, whose sensitiveness had been the cause of many a duel, imagined that the poor animal was making faces at his large nose. He grew excited and drew his sword. Thereupon the monkey, for whom this was a well-rehearsed trick, drew forth his tiny wooden weapon in imitation. Cyrano was infuriated beyond reason and rushing at the creature he killed it with his sword. All Paris heard of the event and an anonymous pamphlet was published concerning it in 1655 called "Combat de Cyrano de Bergerac contre le singe de Brioché."

Another amusing tale is told of an Italian showman, supposed to have been Brioché himself, who wandered into Switzerland where puppets had seldom been seen. There this venturesome fellow narrowly escaped being burned at the stake by the simple-minded inhabitants who swore they had heard the little figures jabber, hence knew they were little devils summoned by evil methods to do their master's bidding. He, poor man, was compelled to save his life by stripping the puppets naked and displaying before his judges their small crude bodies of wood and rags and paper.

However, in France the puppet show gained such popularity and fame that in 1669 Brioché was summoned to the court to amuse the royal Dauphin, son of Louis XIV. Thus Polichinelle makes his bow in the palace as the records of the royal accounts attest: "A Brioché, joueur de marionettes, pour le séjour qu'il a fait à Saint Germain en Laye pendant les mois de septembre, octobre et novembre pour divertir les Enfants de France, 1365 livres." The following year a French showman, Francesco Datelin, was similarly summoned to entertain the Dauphin with his puppets, "à raison de 20 livres par jour." The royal interest in marionettes extended still farther for, some years later, Francesco Brioché and his little wooden figures were protected by a special order of the King himself to the Lieutenant General of Police. And indeed, they probably needed such protection, for their popularity seems to have stirred up enmity against them. Besides they were often meddlesome and impertinent and deserved the wrath they incurred.

Under such favorable conditions companies of marionettes sprang up all over France. They attracted the attention of many writers of the day in whose works we may find them often and favorably mentioned, Gacon, Scarron, La Bruyère, Lemierre, Arnaud. Most ambitious among the immediate successors of the Briocci was the French showman, Bertrand, with his audacious puppets who never hesitated to poke their wooden noses into matters of gravest import. The revocation of the Edict of Nantes furnished one well known occasion. The puppets took sides, representing Catholics and Protestants upon their little stages. Pantalone was in one faction, Harlequin in another and Polichinelle, as Ferrigni describes him, "always something of an unbeliever, is ready at all times to pour ridicule upon the hypocrisy of bigots and the libertism of reformers." The play drew crowds of all classes until it was finally stopped by the authorities who had been notified of it in this manner: "To M. de la Raynie, Councillor of the King in Council. It is said this morning at the Palace that the marionettes at the Fair of Saint Germain are representing the destruction of the Huguenots and, as you will probably find this a serious matter for the marionettes, I have deemed it right to give you the information thereof so that you may make use of it according to your discretion." But despite an occasional rebuff, the marionettes became more and more firmly established in the two Fairs of Saint Laurent and Saint Germain. What clever shows, what ingenious and indefatigable showmen! Bienfait, Gillot, Tiquet, Maurice, De Selles, Francesco Bodinière, the brothers Ferron at *The Sign of the Giglio*, the *Théâtre des Pygmées* of La Grille, the show in the Rue Marais du Temple, *Il Gallo* and many others.

Now indeed the emboldened fantoches began to wage a most amazing battle royal, their opponents being no other than the managers, actors and singers of the contemporary stage. The three great theatres alone at this time had the privilege of representing musical opera, tragedy, or commedie nobili. The puppets were restricted to mere farces of one scene for not more than two characters, only one of whom was allowed to speak and that "par le sifflet, de la pratique," a little contrivance which the showman put into his mouth when reciting to produce the shrill squeak characteristic of Polichinelle from time immemorial. But these showmen circumvented such limitations with many devices, — pantomimes with musical interludes and figures with printed cards hung up to explain the action, even living children combined with puppet play.

The large marionettes of La Grille, manipulated by wires sliding on rails and held upright by weights and counterweights, were claimed by their owner to be a new invention, despite the fact that similar dolls were not unusual in Italy. At any rate they were a novelty in France and to them King Louis XIV accorded special privileges. Nevertheless before long they had over-stepped them and trespassed upon the rights of the actors of the opera. The latter complained to the King. He issued fresh interdictions. The marionettes subsided: only to break forth again. In 1697 the Italian actors in the *Hôtel de Bourgogne* incurred disfavor at court and were temporarily put out of their theatre. Bertrand immediately installed his puppets in triumph upon their vacated stage which he, in turn, was eventually enjoined to quit by a subsequent order of the King. Thus the struggle continued.

In 1720 further privileges were obtained by the marionettes, six or seven at a time being allowed to sing, dance or recite upon the stage. Immediately the famous showman, Francisque, engaged three prominent poets to write new plays for his burattini, Fuzilier, Lesage, and d'Orneval. They set about creating a quite new form of dramatic art, a master stroke which has persisted ever since, the well known *opéra comique*. The first one, *L'ombre du cocher poète*, was given in a booth in the Foire Saint Germain and was so enthusiastically received that the jealous antagonism of directors and singers of the opera was aroused more violently than ever, but the opéra comique remained popular. Piron composed for the burattini an opéra bouffe, La Place, Dolet, Carolet, all invented puppet parodies on the plays and actors of the day. Favert composed his first drama for the pupazzi and Valois d'Orville inaugurated the *Revues de fin d'année*, a criticism of the year's dramatic production by the mocking marionettes.

The seventeenth and eighteenth centuries are quite rightly called the golden age of marionettes. The puppets were executed and managed with utmost skill, the mise-en-scène imitated the magnificence of the larger theatres. The greater the impertinences the greater the popularity of the puppets, — what wonder that the Comédie Française complained of them as a "concurrence déloyale." But with the entrance into the puppet shows of the spectacular, the decline of the French marionettes began. It is true that despite his crude and rather broad repartee so popular in the two fairs, his jokes of doubtful taste relished upon the boulevards, Polichinelle continued to be the vogue among the upper classes. He was called to perform in the salon of the Duc de Bourbon, of the Duc de Bourgogne, of the Duchesse de Berry, and of the Duc de Guise at Meudon. At one time, indeed, the Duchesse de Maine had a puppet stage built at her chateau of Sceaux and plays and epigrams written for it by her friend and secretary, the academician Malezieu, which finally involved an altercation between Polichinelle and the Academy. At the same Castle of Sceaux in 1746 the Comte d'Eu had a company of marionettes brought in and he operated and spoke for them himself. Voltaire, present at this occasion, forgot his quarrel with the burattini for having poked fun at his *Mérope* and *Oreste* and took a hand himself at the manipulating. Eventually he found himself composing for them and inviting them into his own castle, Cirey, where he may have learned many things about the traditional Italian drama from studying the personaggi of the puppet stage.

At this time, indeed, Fourre, Beaupré, Audinot, Nicolet and Servandoni were making lasting names for themselves as directors of marionette theatres but it gradually came to pass that, as the audiences grew cold, witty jests were replaced by spectacular surprises such as the mechanical triumphs achieved by the puppets of Bienfait. We read of M. Pierre's show. "Here are to be seen in every detail, mountains, castles, marine views; also figures that perfectly imitate all natural movements without being visibly acted upon by any string, storm, rain, thunder, vessels perishing, soldiers swimming." We hear of Audinot's exhibition of life-sized *bamboches* imitating with striking resemblance celebrities of the day, displaying the follies and vices of the eighteenth century courts. Children were seen acting with pup-

MARIONETTES

pets and there were innumerable military pieces such as, *The Bombardment of Antwerp*, or *The Taking of Charleroi*. Poor Polichinelle, indeed! We will scarcely be surprised to find him struggling along as best he can and finally suffering a last indignity by losing his little wooden head for the edification of the Parisian mob on the very day, at the very hour, when the unfortunate monarch Louis XVI was guillotined.

Everywhere puppets have originated among the common people: they are primarily an expression of popular taste. Nevertheless, this rude show of the masses has frequently aroused the curiosity of artists and some of them have found in the very naïveté of the dolls unexpected artistic possibilities. The delightful potentialities have been developed into an exquisite and unique art genre in many countries, particularly in France.

We have seen the kings and courts entranced by the burattini of Brioché and his followers. Lesage, Piron and other dramatists were engaged in writing plays for the fantoches; even the great Voltaire entertained his distinguished guests at Cirey with his own puppet shows. Rousseau was interested in them. Gounod wrote "The Funeral March of a Marionette." Charles Magnin, learned member of the Académie Française, devoted himself to the task of chronicling the long history of puppetry. Charles Nodier, persistent visitor of the Parisian shows, is called by some Polichinelle's laureate for the many sparkling pages in his works that are devoted to the marionette.

We shall not be so greatly surprised, therefore, to learn that George Sand had her own puppet theatre at her estate, Nohant, where for thirty years she herself arranged the plays and dressed the dolls while her son, Maurice, sculptured them and acted as director. It was called, *Théâtre des amis* and the first performance was given in 1847. This was a very crude affair got up by Maurice Sand and Eugene Lambert (painter of cats) for themselves and a circle of intimate friends. The stage itself was merely a chair with its back turned to the audience, a cardboard frame arranged in front of it with a curtain to be rolled up and down. The operator knelt upon the seat of the chair, on his hands were placed the puppets, which consisted merely of dresses hung upon sticks of wood for the head, scarcely carved at all. Being tremendously successful, this performance was followed by others. Thus the theatre grew.

George Sand developed very decided theories about her little dolls. She writes that she prefers the sort which may be manipulated on three fingers to those moved by means of wires. Her feeling was that when she thrust her hands into the empty skirts of the inanimate puppet it became alive with her soul in its body, the operator and puppet completely one. She disapproved of realistic puppets. The faces of her dolls were carved with great skill but purposely left crude, painted in oil without varnish to get the strongest effect, with real hair and beards and special attention given to getting light into the eyes. There

GEORGE SAND'S PUPPET THEATRE AT NOHANT
[From Ernest Maindron's *Marionettes et Guignols*]

were, eventually, over one hundred dolls including such as Pierrot, Guignol, Gendarme, Isabelle della Spade, Capitaine, also well known types and personages of the day. Very popular and subsequently famous was the *Green Monster* at Nohant. It appears that in one of the early plays the cast called for a green monster. Upon the maker of the marionettes devolved the task of supplying one. Madame Sand, nothing daunted, discovered an old felt slipper. By using the opening as the wide jaws of the dragon and lining it with red to represent the inside of the mouth, a very effective, long snout was presented which, with a hand slipped inside, could be opened and closed most fearfully and threateningly. It was a highly successful *green monster*. Whenever it appeared there was much applause, and nobody ever seemed to notice or to care that it had been manufactured out of *blue* felt.

The repertoire of the Théâtre des amis was varied, sometimes fantastic whimsies, sometimes travesties on daily events; sometimes the managers grew ambitious and presented spectacular scenes with ballets; the literary side of the production was always emphasized. These shows, the best of their sort, continued through most troublesome times of political upheaval and George Sand has written some touching paragraphs upon the fact that hearts sorely grieved by these national trials, could find distraction and a moment's respite with the marionettes.

The puppets, too, had their vicissitudes. At one

time, Victor Borie, who was assisting, in attempting to represent a fire, burnt down the whole stage. It was built up anew with more puppets and better equipment. Madame Sand dressed the new dolls as she had the old. More helpers had to be called in, all talented persons who entered into the work with enthusiasm. The audience always contained celebrated people, representatives of literature, art, music and statesmanship. Once when the puppets presented a parody upon *La Dame aux Camellias* (presumably not for young ladies) Dumas, fils, came to see and enjoy the production. In 1880 the puppets moved from Nohant to Passy to the home of Maurice Sand, where a large theatre had been prepared for them. Here there were over four hundred elaborate dolls. But in 1889 Maurice Sand died and the Théâtre des amis disappeared. A book written about it was published in 1890.

Equally illustrious and possibly more exquisite, more precious, were the puppets of the *Erotikon theatron de la rue de la Santé*, established in 1862. Here it is said puppetry was raised to an ideal level. Here, an enthusiastic press of the day proclaimed, here was the proof of how highly developed a naïve and simple art may become in the hands of rare spiritual and æsthetic personalities. Another journal, *Le Boulevard*, exclaimed, "Again a new theatre! An intimate theatre, Erotikon theatron, that is to say *Theatre of Amorous Marionettes*. Reassure yourselves, everything that transpires is most conven-

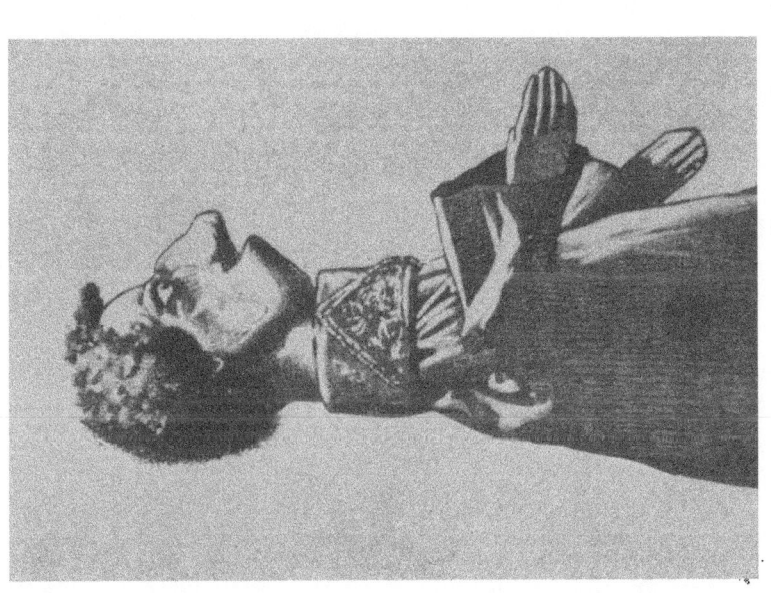

Puppets of George Sand's Theatre at Nohant
[From Ernest Maindron's *Marionettes et Guignols*]

MARIONETTES

tional; the blows of the cudgel are always protectors of morality and if a mother would not see fit to bring her daughter, on the other hand, painters and literateurs of talent take delight in it."

It was indeed an exceptional experiment, a gathering of artists, sculptors, musicians, actors, authors; Lemercier de Neuville, the guiding spirit, assisted in his efforts by Carjat and Gustave Doré, and also by Amedée Rolland, Jean Dubois, Henri Monnier, Théodore de Banville, Bizet, Poulet Malasses, Champfleury, Duranty, Henri Dalage and others, each contributing something toward the perfection of the whole. M. Lemercier de Neuville was in the beginning architect, mason, painter, machinist, carpenter, decorator, hairdresser and tailor, actor, singer, dancer and imitator. Alfred Delvau has written an entertaining history of this bizarre little theatre. The project seems to have been suggested informally at the home of M. Amedée Rolland, by a group of distinguished men of letters who had been lunching together, among them De Neuville, who proceeded to transform the idea thus lightly suggested into a concrete reality.

The auditorium seated only twenty people; its walls were painted with mural decorations by artists of the group, as was the proscenium arch of the stage. The stage itself was only a trifle over two yards wide, but it was well equipped for the presentation of quite elaborate faeries. For the most part, however, there were merely the pupazzi upon the stage, which M.

de Neuville worked himself upon his fingers. Their faces were modelled with unsurpassed refinement and animation, their creator having lavished his heart and talent in the making of them. His *Pierrot Guitariste* was, according to Maindron, the most charming of all puppets, in gesture and bearing a masterpiece of mechanical and plastic art. Others have called it the most highly perfected puppet ever created. Another remarkable doll was the violoncellist who could enter, bow in one hand, instrument in the other, seat himself, tune up and play. There was a Spanish dancer particularly graceful and alluring as well as a wonderful ballet, worked on one horizontal string, which glided in and out and back and forth. Sarah Bernhardt was represented among these fascinating pupazzi and Jules Simon, Coquelin, cadet, and other celebrities familiar in Paris. As de Neuville lived among the individuals he was representing what wonder that his mimicry was close to perfection?

This altogether rare little theatre unfortunately endured for only a year and produced in all but six or seven delightful if slightly shocking pieces, although more had been written for it. Perhaps the dissimilarity of talents comprising it was too great, but at least its inspired cynicisms, amusing audacities and exquisite spectacles have won the lasting acclamations of the French press, of royalty and of the greatest geniuses of the day.

In the shadow play, as well as in the play of pupazzi, French artists have attained great successes.

 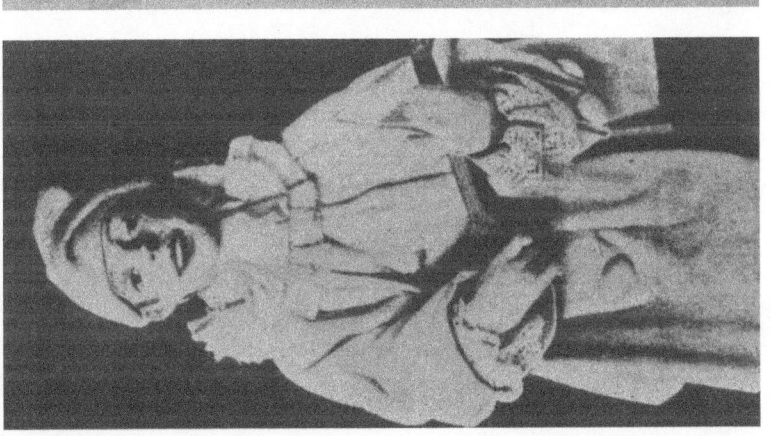 

Sivori. Pierrot Guitariste. Coquelin Cadet
Puppets of Lemercier de Neuville, Erotikon theatron de la rue de la Santé
[Reproduced from Ernest Maindron's *Marionettes et Guignols*]

The first *Ombres Chinoises*, so called, of importance started simply enough about 1770 when Dominique Seraphin, a young man of twenty-three, established his little show in Versailles. In the beginning for the amusement of children, little comical dialogues such as *The Broken Bridge*, or *The Imaginary Invalid* (from Molière), were presented by silhouette figures with articulated limbs. In 1774 after a few years of unusual success, Seraphin moved to Paris where, under royal protection, his little shadows became very well established. Although they had been ensconced in the Palais Royal by favor of the king yet they managed through the cleverness of Seraphin to sustain themselves in popular favor after the overthrow of royalty. Indeed they were said to be the first to avail themselves of advertisements in the form of posted placards.

The advertisement was rather charming:

"Venez, garçon, venez fillette,
Voir Momus à la silhouette.
Qui, chez Seraphin, venez voir
La belle humeur en habit noir.
Tandis que ma salle est bien sombre
Et que mon acteur n'est que l'ombre
Puisse, Messieurs, votre gaîté
Devenir la réalité."

Long after the death of Seraphin, until 1870 in fact, the show continued in the hands of his descendants, presenting pieces especially written for it, with music composed to accompany the shadows.

It was the art critic, Paul Eudel, who first published an illustrated volume of such fairy pieces and melodramas composed by his grandfather in the first quarter of the nineteenth century. Half a century later Lemercier de Neuville, who was interested in *pupazzi noir* as well as in other puppets, published another collection of little plays with fifty illustrations and with explanations of designs and methods of producing the shadows. De Neuville had enlarged the scope but had not changed the principles of the art. He presented animals who opened their jaws, processions and caricatures of celebrities such as Sarah Bernhardt, Zola, and others.

Then a little later came the wonderful shadows, now designated as *Ombres Françaises*, and shown at the Chat Noir, famous cabaret of Montmartre where gathered literary and artistic Bohemia. "The Chat Noir has an art of its own," writes Anatole France, "that is at once mystic and impious, ironical, sad, simple and profound, but never reverential. It is epic and mocking in the hands of the precise Caran d'Ache. It has a bland and melancholy viciousness in Willette, who is, as it were, the Fra Angelico of the cabarets. It is symbolic and naturalistic with the very capable Henri Rivière. The forty scenes of the "Tentation" of St. Anthony amaze me. They exhibit lovely coloring, daring fancy; impressive beauty and forcible meaning. I put them far above the imps depicted by the austere Callot." These comedies, spectacles, military epics, oratorios,

TABLEAU
From a shadow play of *The Prodigal Son* at the Chat Noir
[Designed by Henri Rivière]

MARIONETTES

mysteries, Greek scenes, burlesques and pantomimes, were indeed conceived with a certain large poetic glamour. It was Caran d'Ache who made the great artistic contribution of giving up articulation of individual figures, for the most part, to move great numbers of them along. He invented perspective in shadows, using masses of figures in different planes and producing a sense of solidarity and immensity. His masterpiece, *Epopée*, the evocation of the Grand Army of Napoleon, presented with epic grandeur company after company of cuirassiers in long lines, the profiles diminishing in height as the figures receded from the eyes. It conveyed, as one critic avers, the idea of great space and of a vast army of men marching in serried ranks "to victory or to death." A few single figures were allowed to stand out distinctly like the Little Corporal on horseback, there was little speech only music and an occasional command. The effect of this military silhouette was most impressive.

Next came Henri Rivière, who added the variety of color to the shadows, and furthermore, by the use of two magic lanterns, created dissolving views so that the background might be altered at will. The subjects of his elaborate pantomimes were such as *The Wandering Jew, The Prodigal Son,* and *The Temptation of St. Anthony.* Of the latter, Rehm has given us an admiring appreciation. "We saw the sun setting into the sea, the forests trembling in the morning breeze; we saw deserts stretching out into the infinite, the oceans surging, great cities flaming up in the evening with artificial lights and the moon silvering the ripples of the rivers upon which barges were silently and slowly gliding along. He (Rivière) employs everything from the picturesque style of watercolor spread on with a brush to the imitation of Japanese color prints, pen sketch and poster style, Gothic or Pre-Raphaelite characteristics and naturalistic impressionism. In *The Sphinx* where the conquerors of all centuries, from the Pharaohs to Napoleon, file past this monument of eternity; in his *March of the Stars* where shepherds and their flocks, beggars, slaves and fishermen, and the Wise Men from the East make their pilgrimage to the Virgin with the Divine Child; in the *Enfant Prodigue* where the son of the patriarch sets out for Egypt accompanied by his herds, his caravan, his riders, — to return, a beggar,— everywhere we see this art, dreamlike and philosophic, legendary, fantastic, sublime, creating ecstatic illusions." Of *The Sphinx*, a collaboration of Rivière and Caran d'Ache, Jules Lemaître writes, "Here we have a true epic poem, simple yet grandiose."

Thus the magic touch of genius has transformed naïve shadows into something altogether wonderful while crude pupazzi, animated with thumb and fingers of the artist, have grown gloriously sophisticated. The marionettes that are moved by wire or string also had their renaissance in the sympathetic, stimulating atmosphere of Paris. Their technical development J. M. Petite has called a veritable triumph of

MARIONETTES

ingeniousness, of prestidigitation, and of mechanics. The first of the *Operator-Magicians* was Thomas Holden, who came to Paris around 1875. His puppets performed the most perilously difficult feats. Following in his footsteps came two brothers who rivalled him in skill; Alfred and Charles de Saint-Genois, who took the names of Dickson and John Hewelt respectively. The puppets of Dickson are said to have operated as if by magic. They were mute and appeared on the stage singly, but the perfect elasticity and the winged grace of their gestures seemed truly supernatural. They were displayed at the celebrated theatre of Robert Houdin.

John Hewelt gave productions of quite a different nature. He constructed not only a marionette stage for his actors, but an orchestra of puppets with an animated little leader, and diminutive spectators in the front boxes, a little lady with an opera glass, another with a fan, perfectly gowned in the latest fashions, applauding or chatting after the approved manner. Upon the stage appeared startlingly lifelike figures impersonating Yvette Guilbert and other celebrated actresses and actors of the day. Hewelt stood concealed on a platform overlooking and manipulated his puppets by three controls, with his feet as well as his hands. But despite his unsurpassed inventiveness, his production did not quite satisfy the spirit. One marvelled at the difficulties overcome more than at the beauty of the performance.

As ingenious mechanically as the shows of John

Hewelt and Dickson, but conceived and carried out in a far more inspired and artistic manner, were the puppets of the Galérie Vivienne. *Le Petit Théâtre de M. Henri Signoret* (1888–1892) has been immortalized in the writings of Anatole France, most rare and delicate critic. It was an undertaking seriously entered upon by some of the artistic spirits in Paris who desired to witness intelligent and sympathetic performances of the classic drama of all lands; Greek plays, the mysteries of the Middle Ages, Italian and Spanish comedy of the sixteenth century. Apparently the stage of the day did not satisfy this desire. After encountering insurmountable difficulties in assembling an adequate cast of good actors, it was decided to use marionettes. Forty friends, all artists, combined to help the director, who was the fastidious literateur, M. Signoret. The result was a brilliant success.

The theatre was like a little jewel case in its delicate detail; it seated only two hundred and fifty people. The puppets were most carefully constructed. The same skeleton framework was used for them all but individual heads, hands and chests were put on each frame which was finally costumed according to design. Both the modelling of the faces and the costuming were the inspired creations of artists. The marionettes were moved on rails in grooves or slides, the arms and neck being wired and manipulated by pedals from underneath. The audience was seated low so that the mechanism was invisible. The public who patronized this marionette theatre, indeed, consisted of such interesting people as Jules Lemaître, Émile Faguet, Anatole France, Hugues Leroux, and they were unanimous in their approval. The repertoire included classic drama of every epoch: *The Birds* by Aristophanes, *Abraham* by the Abbess Hrotswitha, *Gardien Vigilant* by Cervantes, *The Tempest* by Shakespeare, *Tobie* and *The Legend of St. Cecelia* by M. Boucher, *L'Amour dans les Enfers* by Amédée Pigeon written expressly for the marionettes of M. Signoret.

But let the fluent pen of the illustrious and enthusiastic witness picture them to you. "I have already made the avowal," declares Anatole France, "I love the marionettes and those of M. Signoret please me particularly. These marionettes resemble the Egyptian hieroglyphics, that is to say, something mysterious and pure and when they represent a drama of Shakespeare or Aristophanes I think I see the thoughts of the poet being unrolled in sacred characters upon the walls of the temple." Of the representation of *The Tempest* he writes: "M. Signoret's marionettes have just acted Shakespeare's *Tempest*. It is hardly an hour since the curtain of the little theatre fell on the harmonious group of Ferdinand and Miranda. I am still under the charm; as Prospero says, 'I do yet taste some subtleties of the Isle.' What a delightful play! And how true it is that exquisite things are doubly exquisite when they are unaffected . . .

"Look at the marionettes of *The Tempest*. The

hand that carved them imprinted on them the features of the ideal, whether it be tragic or comic. M. Belloc, a pupil of Mercie, has modelled for the little theatre heads which are either powerfully grotesque or of a charming purity. His Miranda has the subtle grace of a figure of the early Italian Renaissance and the virginal fragrance of that fortunate fifteenth century which made beauty bloom a second time in the world. His Ariel in his gauze tunic spangled with silver reminds one of a miniature Tanagra figure, doubtless because aerial elegance of form is a particular attribute of Hellenic art in its decline.

"These two pretty puppets spoke with the clear voices of Mesdemoiselles Paule Verne and Cecile Dorelle. As for the more masculine parts in the drama, Prospero, Caliban, and Stephano, poets such as MM. Maurice Bouchor, Raoul Ponchan, Amédée Pigeon, Felix Rabbé spoke for them. Not to mention Coquelin, cadet, who did not disdain to repeat the prologue as well as the amusing part of Trinculo, the clown.

"The decorations also had their poetry. M. Lucien Doucet represented Prospero's cave with that cunning grace which is one of the characteristics of his talent, etc."

Again: "In the meantime I have seen the marionettes of the Rue Vivienne twice and I have enjoyed them very much. I am infinitely thankful to them for having replaced living actors.

"They are divine, these dolls of M. Signoret and

worthy of giving form to the dreams of the poet whose mind Plato says, was 'the sanctuary of the Graces.'

"Thanks to them we have Aristophanes in miniature. When the curtain has risen on an aerial landscape and we have watched the two semicircles of birds taking their places on either side of the sacrifice, we have formed some idea of the theatre of Bacchus. What a delightful representation! One of the two leaders of the birds turning to the spectators utters these words: 'Feeble men, like unto the leaf, vain creatures fashioned out of clay and wanting wings, unhappy mortals condemned to an ephemeral and fugitive life, shadows, baseless dream . . .' It is the first time, I think that marionettes have spoken with this melancholy gravity."

All this is very interesting and very serious, no doubt, but what of the piping, impertinent voice of Polichinelle? And of this merry Guignol who makes the children laugh? It may seem odd to insert these slapstick buffoons into the midst of aristocratic literary puppets, but after all Guignol was growing and thriving contemporaneously with them and the hardy little fellow has outlived the most of them. Less elaborate and socially less select than those others installed in their artistic theatres, these al fresco performances in the Champs Élysées, in the gardens of the Tuileries and Luxembourg follow the traditional custom of their kind. The *castellet* of Guignol is little different from Punch's booth, the dolls are most often simple creatures worked on the fingers, squeaking extemporary dialogue such as one might hear from the pupazzi of Italy or the figures of the Chinese peripatetic showman swathed in his linen bag.

Polichinelle has been through difficult times. The French Revolution found him obscure but a patriot, rejoicing at the new order of things. Later he was discovered amusing Emperor Napoleon the Third at the Tuileries Palace. In 1854 the French Zouaves and Grenadiers in the Crimea took Polichennello along with them and he loyally followed up to the very battlefield. But oftenest he was to be seen, through the long lapse of years, humilated, humbled, — dancing on a board at the twitch of a horizontal string tied to the knee of some little Savoyard boy who beat a tambourine or blew upon a pipe and sang a pathetic song as he journeyed on to Paris. And there, too, on sidewalks and, when the wind blew cold, in the shelter of arches puppets danced on the board and the little boy gathered his pennies to send back home to his mother.

Thus Polichinelle has pursued his incredible career until we find him to-day with a devoted wife La Mère Gigogne and many well known if less popular fellows, such as Pierrot, and Harlequin, to say nothing of his many delightful and successful offspring. There is Lafleur the Polichinelle of Picardy, favorite of Amiens, a handsome peasant fellow always pleasant spoken even when beating up the policeman. Jacques is a little buffoon who entertains the public of Lille in his modest basement theatre. There in *Joseph sold by his Brothers*, or *Ali Baba and the Forty Thieves* he performs the principal parts ("la comédie pour un sou"). Most prominent of the progeny of Polichinelle is Guignol. Indeed he somewhat overshadows his sire.

Although he has established himself so thoroughly in Paris Guignol first came from Lyons. His creator was the modest but expert marionettist, Laurent Mourguet. It is he who is reported to have said to the friends weeping at his deathbed, "I shall never make you cry as much as I have made you laugh." Guignol originated in a picturesque but humble cellar show. Although he has now moved into new and finer quarters, he remains a modest workman simply dressed, perpetually harried by his landlord and always with insufficient funds to pay his rent. He has a wife, long suffering *Madelon*, and a wild and wicked son *Guillaume* and along with them one finds *Gnaffron, Gringellet, Bobine, Bambochnette, le Gendarme, le Médecin, le Propriétaire, le Juge*, all these and many others.

In the Gardens of the Luxembourg, on the Champs Élysées or elsewhere in Paris, one may come upon these little actors merrily performing on small stages erected for them, and with an audience of spell-bound children and nursemaids sitting before the castellet.

Most celebrated of these Parisian theatres is that of the *Vrai Guignol* in the Champs Élysées. M. Anatole, the founder of it, was the first who undertook to expand the repertoire of Guignol and to introduce pieces of adventure whose very names delight one: *The Brigands of the Black Forest, The Enchanted Village, Mother Michel and her Cat, The Temptation of St. Anthony,* and many more. Unfortunately for M. Anatole there was no copyright law for puppet plays and when a rival showman wanted to give a new play he merely went to see Anatole's performance and then reproduced it. But Anatole himself deserves his reputation. He was an artist with prodigious ingenuity: he wrote his own pieces, he could give twenty distinct voices in one show as well as manipulate the dolls. He himself carved the puppets' heads while his wife made the costumes.

Inspired by his success a young literateur, Charles Duranty, attempted in 1862 to *uplift* Guignol. He had an elegant little castellet erected and he spent months preparing the plays, giving them style and some sort of philosophical turn. His figures were created by artists. The prologue, it is said, was composed by a poet. The result was — a failure. His show appealed to too limited an audience; it was too artistic for the nursemaids and soldiers. The Tuileries were not for philosophy. The scenes soon were left to Guignol and the Commissaire who are so dear and delightful to their Parisian public. And again recently, a version of Rostand's *Chantecler* was given by the puppets. There were to be seen chickens, peacocks, dogs, even a magnificent rooster, but Guignol and Guillaume were wanting. Surprised at first,

MARIONETTES

before long the children began to clamor for their heroes, — and they had to be satisfied.

On the steamship La France, now sailing back and forth across the ocean, one may find a little theatre for Guignol in the children's room. It is operated every day by Paul Boinet who is considered one of the best Guignol experts in France and was specially engaged by the French Line for that reason. He operates plays, we are told, in which there are sometimes as many as fifteen actors and to each puppet's voice he manages to give a different intonation. The children's room of the steamer holds about fifty people and is filled to capacity at each performance not only with children but with grown-up people.

Meanwhile literary puppets continue to afford pleasure in the artistic salons or in semi-public productions throughout Paris. It would be vain to attempt to mention them all. They are of every type. The artists of France have the *habit* of the marionette, they express themselves spontaneously and gladly in this métier and hence we find them giving more or less informal presentations of poetic or satiric drama here and there, from year to year. M. Émile Renie had *le théâtre des marionettes de la Rue des Martyrs;* Cayot established a *théâtre des pupazzi* in his photographic studio. At the Paris Exposition of 1900 there flourished a marionette theatre with a troupe of 4,000 dolls of whom the leading actors were marvels of mechanical perfection. Quite recently a show was installed at the Musée Grevin with decorations by

Jules Cheret. It was not a great financial success and was obliged to close its doors. In 1896 in the Salons of *la Plume*, Lugné Poë (Director of L'Œuvre) produced a marionette play of Alfred Jarry and Claude Terrasse entitled *Ubu Roi*. The former also made the drawings for two programmes, the latter was the leader of his orchestra.

Jules Lemaître in his *Impressions de Théâtre* portrays with great interest several puppet productions witnessed by him. One was the chic Revue in four tableaux given in 1889 at the Salon de Helder by the well known authoress, Gyp. It was called *Tout à l'égout*, a very clever and original parody of the season past. There Gyp had represented the type for which she has grown famous, Lou-lou the pert little French miss as seen on the Champs Élysées. There also promenaded the literary and political celebrities satirized in the inimitable style of the keen-eyed Gyp. The parts were read by amateurs, effectively but with no attempt at eloquence.

Very different in spirit was the puppet drama, *Noël ou le Mystère de la Nativité*, by the poet Maurice Bouchor who had been active also in the Erotikon theatron and that of M. Signoret. It was written in four tableaux, in verse. The music for this delicate little mystery was composed by Paul Vidal, the dolls were designed by MM. Henri Lombard and J. Belloc, scenery by Félix Bouchor, brother of the poet, Henri Lerolle and Marcelle Rieder. Lemaître described the performance as a masterpiece of grace and

GUIGNOL AND GNAFRON
Presented by Pierre Rousset, French showman
[From Ernest Maindron's *Marionettes et Guignols*]

MARIONETTES

beauty, particularly the last tableau of the Adoration. "The music of the lullaby, rarely exquisite, soft and celestial, etc. The Virgin puppet, almost immobile, merely inclining slightly forward toward the Infant while singing, had the candor of a lily and appeared as beautiful in the light in which she was bathed as the purest and most naïve Virgin of the primitive painters." Another play by the same poet was given in 1894. It was in verse, five tableaux. M. Lemaître considered it even superior as a drama to *Noël* though possibly a bit strong for the puppets in its philosophy. It was the last performance, unfortunately, of the "delicious marionettes of Maurice Bouchor."

The latest word I have heard of French puppets comes from the war zone. Mr. Henry S. West has written in a recent number of the *Literary Digest* of French troops in the forests of Champenoux and Parroy who had taken an oath "never to retreat from Lorraine." Hence they have made themselves a comfortable park with flower beds, gravel paths, rustic bench, all in their *Parc des Braves*. Most diverting, however, are their elaborately constructed scenes of puppet warfare. The most famous of these is *The Seven Chasseurs of Domèvre*. It appears that seven French soldiers at Domèvre held a bridge against a small horde of Germans. It was a brave deed which resounded through Lorraine. Some clever lad wrote several stanzas about it and tacked them up on trees. This gave the idea to a dramatic critic who was off active duty for the time. He and his friends worked together and in a week completed the little show and placed it where it could be seen by every soldier passing on his way to battle.

A grassy knoll was chosen. An arched bridge of two feet was erected under which real water was made to flow. On one side of the bridge were piled tiny logs and trees behind which were the seven Chasseurs eight inches high dressed in the old red and blue French uniform, little caps on their heads, wooden guns in their hands. Twenty Germans in real field-grey were attempting to charge. Some were dead, others falling, three running away, all with scared expressions carved upon their little wooden faces. The verses were nailed up near by:

"There were seven Chasseurs of Domèvre
Who were so exceedingly brave
When the Germans attacked
They got thoroughly whacked,
'Voila!' said the men of Domèvre."

Puppet Shows of Germany and of Other Continental Countries

PERHAPS it was the luxuriant forests of Germany offering abundant material and opportunity which encouraged the native aptitude, at any rate the inhabitants of the land have at all times been noted for their skill in wood carving. Moreover they appear to take a certain delight in mechanical devices. From very early times these interests were applied to the making of mechanical toys and dramatic puppets.

In the dark ages we find the people of the country carving a grotesque sort of wooden doll, called *Kobold* or *Tattermann* which they set up in the chimney and worshipped as a heathen household deity. Later these little figures came to be worked by wires. As far back as the twelfth century and according to Charles Magnin even in the tenth century, the word *Tocha* or *Docha* was used to signify a kind of puppet. One of the earliest Minnesingers mentions *Tokkenspil* in his poem and another speaks of the *Jongleuren* attracting their audiences by displaying little dolls which they pulled out at any time from under their mantles.

The subject of the early Tokkenspiel seems to have been gathered chiefly from the legends of the *Edda,* and from the *Hildebrandslied* and the *Niebelungenlied.* Praetorius mentions: "Foolish jugglers' tents where old Hildebrand and such *Possen* are played with *Dokken,* called puppet comedies." Later the mystery play appeared and the automatic *Kruppenspiel,* religious drama here as elsewhere opening up a path for the profane. These plays were founded upon such themes as, *The Fall of Adam and Eve, Goliath and David, Judith and Holofernes, King Herod* or *The Siege of Jerusalem.*

Of the fourteenth and fifteenth centuries we have little positive data. Romantic subjects appear to have been used for the puppets, also history and fable such as *The Four Sons of Aymon, Genevieve of Brabante, The Lady of Roussillon,* and even *Joan of Arc* which was quoted in another piece performed in 1430.

Invariably the comic element appears in the puppet shows of all nations. In Germany and Austria the buffoon has always been a part of even the most tragic dramas, lending variety and relief by his good natured, if somewhat obvious jests. The first names by which he was known in Germany may have been Meister Eulenspiegel or Hemmerlein, later it became Hanswurst and Kasperle. The name Kasperle, so Rabe claims, came through Austria and Professor Pischel goes still further in his assertion that the prototype for Kasperle was brought into the land over two thousand years ago from India. Later, of course,

MARIONETTES

Italian and French players introduced Pulcinella and Arlecchino with their merry company.

In Hamburg puppets have been popular from earliest times. It was in 1472 that a showman announced *The Public Beheading of the Virgin Dorothea*. This theme remained a favorite in the puppet plays of that city for centuries, while the long suffering martyr continued to be ever more and more elaborately but neatly beheaded, in full view of the audience. In the eighteenth century an announcement proclaimed: "Exceptional marionette players with large figures and, accompanied by lovely singing, the execution of Dorothea." The play of *The Prodigal Son* was another great favorite. It gradually lost its religious character and became a rather gruesome affair producing with ingenious mechanical appliances metamorphoses of which the country has always been particularly fond. For instance, Reibehand, a tailor who set up a booth in the horse market of Hamburg, advertised in 1752: "The Arch-prodigal chastened by the four elements, with Harlequin a joyous companion of the great criminal." This *extra-moral* piece, given in great style, displays the prodigal about to partake of fruit which turns into skulls in his hands, then water becomes transformed into fire, rocks rend apart disclosing a corpse hanging from a gallows. As it swings in the wind, the limbs fall off and then collect again, on the ground, and arise to pursue the prodigal, and so on with similarly pleasing surprises.

In 1688 another showman, Elten, advertised *Adam and Eve* and following it *Jackpudding in a Box* and later another announces: *Elijah's Translation into Heaven*, or *The Stoning of Naboth*, followed by a farce, *The Schoolmaster Murdered by Jackpudding* or *The Baffled Bacon Thieves*.

There had been in Hamburg, however, French marionette troupes which gave very artistic puppet operas based upon mythological subjects, such as *Medea*, including in one of its casts a puppet who smoked! These plays were produced in combination with acts by living actors, jugglers, acrobats, and trick horses.

As far back as the sixteenth century scepticism and sorcery had become the order of the day with the Germans who have naturally a tendency toward philosophical reflections, as well as a leaning toward the occult and supernatural. It was then that *Faust*, embodying both of these tendencies, first appeared upon the puppet stage, with most significant consequences for German literature.

This puppet play might be sufficiently interesting in itself, but the fact that it became the inspiration for one of the world's greatest dramas may lend an added justification for pausing a moment to trace its curious history. Early in the sixteenth century it is said that the Tokkenspieler presented, at the Fairs, *The Prodigious and Lamentable History of Doctor Faustus*. In 1587 the famous *Spiesische Faust Buch* was published in Frankfurt and recorded the adventures of a semi-historical charlatan who had wandered through Germany in the early sixteenth century. He was famous not only for his skill in medicine but in necromancy and other similar arts. He may have been identical with Georgius Sabellicus who called himself Faustus Junior, implying that there had been a still earlier Faust. He may possibly have been the Bishop Faustinus of Diez, seduced from the right path by Simon Magus, or the printer of Mainz, Johann Faust, who was declared to have been a sorcerer. Whoever he was, the disreputable conjurer tricked fate into granting him an immortal name. In 1588 two students of Tübingen and a publisher were punished for putting forth a puppet play based upon this Spies' book. There are other versions of the Faust puppet show, that played at Strassburg, that of Augsburg, of Ulm and of Cologne, each varying slightly from the others. They were all first produced about the time of Marlowe's famous drama on the same theme or only a trifle later.

The story of the Faust play has a tremendous appeal; it is a picture of man's vain desires and vain regrets. We find the scholar Faust alone in his study, meditating over the wasted years of research and the wisdom of this world which is so limited at best. He turns to the black arts and summons up an evil spirit to serve him. In one version of the puppet play Faust calls up numerous devils and decides to select as his own particular servant the swiftest. Thereupon the evil spirits describe their speed. One claims to be "as swift as the shaft of pestilence"; the next is "as swift as the wings of the wind"; another "as a ray of light"; the fourth "as the thought of man"; the fifth "as the vengeance of the Avenger." But the last, who is Mephistopheles, is as swift "as the passage from the first sin to the second." Faust replies: "That is swift indeed. Thou art the devil for me." Then he signs the pact with his blood. A raven flies in and carries away the message. Mephistopheles is bound for twenty-four years to provide Faust with all the pleasures of this world and also *to answer truthfully every question asked him.* In return Faust pledges his soul to the devil at the expiration of the time.

Mephistopheles carries Faust to the court of the Count of Parma where he entertains the count and countess with magical shows, calling up Samson and Delilah, David and Goliath, Solomon and the Queen of Sheba. Throughout the play Faust is always taken seriously; Kasperle supplies the ludicrous element. His buffoonery is at times really amusing. As an assistant of Faust's servant Wagner, he meddles with magic, on his own responsibility. Having picked up a few words of incantation, he uses them according to his own pleasure; but Kasperle is wiser than his master for he very shrewdly refuses to sign away his soul. However, he has discovered that by pronouncing the potent syllables "Perlippe" he can summon up demons and by saying "Perlappe" he can make them vanish. Thereupon he amuses him-

MARIONETTES

self (and the audience) by reciting "Perlippe, perlappe, perlippe, perlappe," so often and in such quick succession that the poor demons get quite out of breath and very irritable.

In the last act we find Faust back after twelve years at his study in Wittenburg. He has had his fill of pleasures and is sick at heart and repentant. He asks Mephistopheles whether there would be a chance of a sinner like himself coming to God. Mephistopheles, compelled by his oath to answer truthfully, vanishes with a cry of terror which is an admission of the possibility. Faust, with new hope in his heart, kneels before the image of the Virgin in supplication. But Mephistopheles reappears with a vision of Helen of Troy to tempt Faust, who resists but finally succumbs. Forgetting the Virgin he rushes out with Helen in his arms. Immediately he returns and reproaches Mephistopheles for deceiving him, because the vision has turned into a serpent in his embrace. "What else did you expect from the devil?" asks Mephistopheles.

Faust realizes he is lost. Moreover his time is up, for the devil having served him both night and day considers that he has done twenty-four years work in twelve. Wandering the streets in despair Faust comes upon Kasperle, now the nightwatchman, and tries naïvely to cheat the devil by offering Kasperle his own coat. But the shrewd fellow is too keen to be thus taken to eternal torture in another's place. Ten o'clock strikes, then eleven. "Go," says Faust to

Kasperle, "go and see not the dreadful end to which I hasten." Kasperle goes out. Twelve o'clock strikes and Faust hears the terrible sentence pronounced upon him: "Accusatus est, judicatus est, condamnatus est." The fiends appear amidst flames and smoke and drag him away to his horrible fate. Kasperle returning and finding him gone, exclaims: "Poof! What a smell of brimstone!"

Even the briefest review of the plot cannot fail to move one somewhat for there is in this crude puppet show a deep and general human appeal. An earnest and anxious man to whom life has not been over-kind stakes all in his eagerness and craving for truth. Despite the naïve superstitions and the childish humor scattered throughout the play the tragic seeking of a human soul, the struggle between Mephistopheles and Faust demands our sympathy. In this respect there is more dramatic intensity and more human interest to the puppet show than one finds in either Marlowe's play or even Goethe's. In the former Faust is pictured with a desire to *possess* and we know that he is lost from the beginning; in Goethe's drama Faust is consumed with a desire to *live* and we know throughout that he will be saved by his very struggles. In the puppet play Faust is finally condemned, but until the very end, by Mephistopheles' own admission, he might have been saved.

The play was tremendously popular all over Germany. In 1705 the puppets got themselves into trouble with the clergy by a performance brought from Vienna to Berlin where it was announced, *Vita, Geste e Descesa all' Inferno del dottore Giovanni Faust.* Because of the storm of approval aroused by the impious passages in the drama the performance was finally prohibited in Berlin. But elsewhere productions of *Faustus* flourished. In 1746 in Hamburg an amusing announcement proceeded to allay the fears of timid folk in the following manner: "History of the Arch-sorcerer Doctor Johannes Fauste. This tragedy is presented by us, *not* so fearfully as it has been previously by others, but so that everyone can behold it with pleasure."

Half a century later Schutz and Dreher, very successful showmen of Berlin with a splendidly equipped puppet stage, presented among numerous old pieces of knightly romance, mythology and biblical legend, the tragedy of *Faust.* It was acclaimed by high and low. Then Geisselbrecht, a rival showman of Vienna, strove to outdo this production and gave an elaborate Faust play with little figures whom he made lift and cast down their eyes, even cough and spit very naturally, — a feat which Kasperle was nothing loath to perform over and over again as we may imagine. It was this very Geisselbrecht who served as a model for *Pole Poppenspäler,* the delightful little novel which Theodor Storm has written around the figure of a wandering puppet showman. Geisselbrecht toured with his puppets and gave performances all over the country, in Frankfurt among other places.

The crowning significance of his *Faust* production was the fact that young Goethe, who was very fond of puppet shows, is supposed to have seen this play and to have drawn from it the first inspiration for his masterpiece, *Faust*.

In his childhood Goethe had always manifested great interest in toy theatres and puppets. At twenty years of age he wrote for his own amusement, *The Festival of Plundersweilen*, a satire on his audience of friends and family to be performed by marionettes. Later he perfected it and produced it on a puppet stage specially erected for the purpose at Weimar. There also he composed another puppet play to celebrate the marriage festivities of Princess Amelia. Both of these dramas are included in his works. In *Wilhelm Meister* and in the *Urmeister* we find many paragraphs devoted to the toy theatre of his childhood. But more important than this was the contribution of the little *Puppen* toward his immortal *Faust*. They not only suggested the theme but offered models for the treatment of it which Germany's great genius was not too proud to follow.[1]

[1] The research of scholars has discovered in the Ulm versions of the Faustspiel the suggestion for the *Prologue in Heaven*, although in the puppet play it was held in the Inferno before Satan, not before Die Padre. *Faust's Monologue* seems patterned after that in the Tübingen play or that of Frankfurt am Main. The metaphysical debate between Faust and Mephistopheles has its prototype in the Augsburg Faustus. The tavern scene may have been drawn from a similar scene in the Cologne play. Similarly the Phantasmagoria of Blocksberg and other arrangements may be traced back to the old puppet show Faust.

MARIONETTES

The unpreceoented prominence of the Puppenspiel during the seventeenth century was brought about by the long theological strife between the clergy and the actors of the legitimate stage. The preachings and denunciátions of Martin Luther had put an end to dramatic church ceremonies of which there seem to have been many. It went so far that the ministers refused to administer the sacraments to actors. The latter protested and appealed, but the people were restrained through their fear of the Church. Consequently the profession fell into such disrepute that the number of regular theatres rapidly decreased and troupes were disbanded, while the humiliated and neglected players were forced to join puppet companies and read for the marionettes to earn a living.

It was a great opportunity for the marionettes. After the Thirty Years' War showmen came into Germany from England, France, Holland, Italy, even from Spain. To add to the attraction of their productions they combined with the plays dancers, jugglers, trained bears and similar offerings. In 1657 in Frankfurt Italian showmen established the first permanent theatre for puppets. In 1667 a similar theatre was erected for marionettes in the Juden Markt of Vienna where it remained for forty years. In Leopoldstadt in the Neu Markt *Pulzinellaspieler* gave performances in the evenings except Fridays and Saturdays, after *angelus domini*. Even the Emperor Joseph II is said to have visited this *Kaspertheater* in Leopoldstadt.

A curious dramatic medley began to be presented.

"At the end of the seventeenth century," writes Flögel, "the *Hauptundstaatsactionen* usurped the place of the real drama." These were melodramatic plays with music and pantomime, requiring a large cast composed partly of mechanical dolls, partly of actors. It was only timidly that the actors thus ventured to return to the stage in the rôles of virtuous people (to be sure of the sympathy of the audience). The famous showmen Beck and Reibehand were noted for these performances, the subjects of which were martyrdoms of saints, the slaughter in the ancient Roman circuses and the gory battles of the Middle Ages (in all of which, needless to say, the puppets performed the parts of the slaughtered and martyred, as when the ever popular *Santa Dorotea* was decapitated and applauded so vigorously that the showman obligingly stepped out, put the head back on the body and repeated the execution). In 1666 in Lüneberg, Michael Daniel Treu gave the following *Demonstratioactionum:* "I: the History of the city of Jerusalem with all incidents and how the city fell is given naturally with marvellous inventions openly presented in the theatre; II: of King Lear of England, a matter wherein disobedience of children against the parent is punished, the obedience rewarded; III: of Don Baston of Mongrado, strife between love and honor, etc., etc." Then there followed in the list of plays *Alexander de Medici, Sigismundo, tyrannical prince of Poland, the Court of Sicily, Titus Andronicus, Tarquino, Edward of England* and,

MARIONETTES

of course, *Doctor Johanni Fausto, Teutsche Comedi* (to distinguish it from Marlowe's tragedy).

When one considers that these plays with all the necessary business were long and complicated, one may imagine the difficulty of the art of puppet showmen. Everything connected with the presentation, the settings, directions and the plays themselves had to be learned by heart. Young boys generally attached themselves to showmen as apprentices and observed and studied for years before they were even allowed to speak parts. These had to be acquired by listening, for although the owner of the puppets generally had a copy of the play it was so precious a possession that he guarded it most carefully.

The amazing repertory of the Puppenspiel during the seventeenth and eighteenth centuries ranged from myth and history to any event of the day of intrinsic interest. In 1688 we find the marionette manager, Weltheim, giving translations of Molière, also the old *Adam and Eve* followed by a buffoonery called *Jack Pudding in Punch's Shop* and the strange assortment of *Asphalides, King of Arabia, The Lapidation of Naboth, The Death of Wallenstein*. Weltheim used students of Jena and Leipsig to read for his puppets.

When in 1780 Charles XII of Sweden fell dead in the trenches of Friedrichschall, slain (so popular tradition averred) by an enchanted bullet, his death was immediately dramatized and produced on the puppet stage. In 1731 the disgrace of Menschikoff was made into a drama performed in German by the English puppets of Titus Maas, privileged comedian of the court of Baden Durlach, — "With permission, etc., etc., there will be performed on an entirely new theatre and with good instrumental music, a Hauptundstaatsaction recently composed and worthy to be seen, which has for title — The Extraordinary vicissitudes of good and bad fortune of Alexis Danielowitz, Prince Menzikoff, great favorite of the Czar of Moscow, Peter I of glorious memory, today a real Belisarius, precipitated from the height of his greatness into the most profound abyss of misfortune; the whole with Jackpudding, a pieman, a pastry-cook's boy and amusing Siberian poachers." Although Titus Maas had permission to perform in Berlin his show was quickly stopped for political reasons.

The undisputed predominance of puppets upon the German stage gradually subsided in the eighteenth century as Gottsched and Lessing revived the art of poetry and drama. The actors assumed their own place in the theatre; the Puppen returned to a more modest sphere. But they continued to be popular. After Schütz und Dreher in Berlin came Adolf Glasheimer's humorous satires of which the hero was *Don Carlos*, with Kasperle to amuse the children, the whole arrangement conducted in connection with a *Conditerei*. In 1851 a revival of marionettes in cultural circles occurred and people streamed to see the clever show in Kellner's Hotel at Christmas time. Richter, Freudenberg and Linde were three other favorite showmen of Berlin.

There had been, indeed, some very exclusive and artistic marionettes at the castle of Eisenstadt in Hungary. Here Prince Nicholas Joseph von Esterhazy had his own very elegant stage with dolls exquisitely perfect and magnificently dressed. He even assembled an orchestra for them, the leader of which was no other than Joseph Haydn himself. This great musician did not scorn composing symphonies for the puppets, *The Toy Symphonies* and *The Children's Fair*, both charmingly playful compositions. He also wrote five operas for these distinguished marionettes, *Filemon and Baucis, Genievre, Didone, Vendetta, The Witches' Sabbath*. But it was not his noble patron alone who influenced Haydn to compose for the puppets. Previously he had become interested and had written an opera called *The Lame Devil* for the burattini of an Italian puppet player, Bernardoni, in Vienna.

The marionettes have likewise attracted genius in other fields. The Romanticists, Arnim and Brentano, as well as the poets Kerner, Uhland and Mörike had interested themselves in shadow plays rather than puppet shows. But Heinrich Kleist wrote a very sympathetic and profound little essay called *Concerning the Marionette Theatre*. He seeks to discover the mysterious charm in puppet gesture and he suggests that the great dramatists must have watched the puppet plays with unusual interest and that artists of the dance might well learn the art of pantomime from the little figures.

In Cologne there has been developed a very unique, local puppet show called the *Kölner Hanneschen Theater*. The originator was Christoph Winter who invented the characters, established the standing theatre and remained for fifty years its director. Upon his small stage there appeared not only Kasperle, but a whole row of funny folk types, mirroring in their little scenes the bubbling love of living characteristic of the people they represent. The ingenious showman had a saying that whatever type of man one had to deal with, give him the sort of sausage he most enjoys. In accordance with this idea he provided three shows, one for children, which was amusing but harmless, one for the usual adult audience, which was more sophisticated, and one especially suited to the rough Sunday crowd of laboring men who thronged into the show, which, needless to say, was as vulgar as possible. Hanneschen, Mariezebill, Neighbor Tünnes and his wife, the village tailor and a host of others were always introduced and furthermore any person in the vicinity who had made himself unpopular was sure to be caricatured. Neither rank nor age was a protection. Another unvarying principle was the happy ending; even *Romeo and Juliet* was altered to comply with the rule.

It is difficult now, perhaps, to think of Munich as it was just before the war, a joyous center of literature and art. It was, however, in this happy environment that the puppets rose to the very summit of their honors and successes. In Munich one may

MARIONETTES

find two charming little buildings which were erected and maintained solely for the marionettes. The oldest of these was built for the old showman, fondly called Papa Schmidt by his devoted public. His career was a long one, terminating with gratifying appreciation which many another worthy marionettist has unfortunately failed to receive. It was in 1858 that the actor, Herr Schmidt, took over a complete little puppet outfit of the retired General von Heydeck who had been entertaining King Louis and his court with satirical little puppet parodies. Installing these dolls in a *Holzbaracke* he opened a permanent theatre there for which Graf Pocci, his constant advisor and friend, wrote the first play based upon the tale of *Prinz Rosenrot und Prinzessin Edelweiss*. Graf Pocci continued all his life to write little fairy plays for these puppets, over fifty in all. The subjects were well known fairy tales, Undine, Rapunzel, Schneewitschen, Der Rattenfänger von Hamlin, Dornröschen, and all the others. The children loved them and the merry little Kasperle whose humor, if a bit clumsy, was altogether clean and wholesome. Encouraged by his initial success, Schmidt went to great expense and pains to enlarge and elaborate his cast. His daughter, an assiduous helper, was kept busy dressing the dolls of which there were eventually over a thousand.

After long years of success, Papa Schmidt experienced some difficulties due to moving his puppet show and decided to retire. To the honor of Munich be it said, however, that he was not allowed to do so. The city magistrates who, as youngsters, had adored the antics of Kasperle, voted unanimously to build a municipal puppet theatre and to rent it to old Papa Schmidt for his marionette shows. This was done and in a small comfortable building situated in one of the parks, with an adequate auditorium and stage, with space for the seven operators who guide the wires and manage the complicated mechanism for *transformations and surprises*, with trained readers to speak the parts behind the scenes, with choruses and music whenever they were required, the ninety-four year old showman worked with his dolls until the end of his life, furnishing happy hours to countless children.

The celebrated *Marionette Theatre of Munich Artists*, although inspired by the example of Papa Schmidt, was founded upon an altogether different basis and with other aims and ideals. Paul Brann, an author of local fame, was the instigator of it as well as its director. This small but elaborate modern theatre was built by Paul Ludwig Troost, and decorated elegantly but with careful taste, by other artists interested in the enterprise. The stage itself is equipped with every possible device useful to any modern theatre. There is a revolving stage such as that used by Reinhardt, and a complicated electrical apparatus which can produce the most exquisite lighting effects. The expensive furniture is often a product of the *Königlichen Porcellan Manufactur*. The mechanism for operating the figures is very perfect, the dolls them-

MARIONETTE THEATRE OF MUNICH ARTISTS
Upper: Scene from Maurice Maeterlinck's *The Death of Tintagiles*
Lower: Scene from Arthur Schnitzler's *The Gallant Cassian*

MARIONETTES

selves as well as the costumes, scenery, curtains, programs, etc., are all designed and executed by well known artists such as Joseph Wackerle and Taschner, Jacob Bradle, Wilhelm Schulz, Julius Dietz and many others. Indeed the scenic effects produced at this little marionette theatre have given it the reputation of a model in modern stagecraft.

The triumphs of these Munich puppets, however, do not depend altogether on pictorial successes. Upon the miniature stage there are presented dramas of the best modern poets as well as the older classic plays and the usual Kasperle comedies. Puppets must remain primitive or they lose their own peculiar charm, but the primitive quality may be ennobled. Brann does not in the least detract from the innate simplicity which the marionettes possess. Indeed, he considers this not a limitation but a distinguishing trait. However, he has added poetic art to the old craft and has expanded the sphere of the puppets. He has proven their poetic possibilities and justified their claim to the consideration of cultured audiences. The repertory has been specially selected to suit his particular dolls, somewhat pantomimic, on the whole, with a great deal of music. Generally the plays deal with incidents unrelated to everyday life and these marionettes convey their audiences with unbelievable magic to arcadian lands of dream and wonder. Graf Pocci's little Kasperle pieces were not scorned by these artistic marionettes nor the old Faustspiel, Don Juan and the Prodigal

Son, nor the folk-plays of Hans Sachs. To these were added a rich variety, including many forgotten operettas of Gluck, Adam, Offenbach, Mozart and others, Schnitzler's *Der Brave Cassian*, Maeterlinck's *Death of Tintagiles*, and *Sister Beatrice*, and dramas of Hoffmansthal. The popularity of these puppet productions in Munich, and their success all over the world, where they have been taken travelling into foreign lands, attest the worth and value of the interesting experiment. For art, music and literature a new medium has been discovered, or rather an old one re-adapted to suit the requirements of the modern poetic drama.

Of recent years the shadow play has not been altogether overlooked in Munich. In a 1909 issue of the *Hyperion*, Franz Blei, æsthete and critic, describes two exquisite shadow plays performed in the salon of Victor Mannheimer. The figures and scenery were the work of a young architect, Höne; actors read the text, and Dr. Mannheimer directed. "One thing," writes Blei, "I believe was clear to all present: that both of the plays thus presented, unhampered by perspiring, laboring and painted living actors, appealed more strongly to the inner ear than they could possibly have done in any other theatre. The author was allowed to express himself, rather than the actor. The stage setting and the outlines of the shadows, very delicately cut in accordance with the essential traits of the characters, presented no more than a delightful resting place for the eye and the imagination of the beholder was unrestricted in supplying the features while lingering on the extreme simplicity of the picture." Elsewhere too in Germany one finds appreciation of the possibilities of the shadow play, in its simplest form as well as in its sophisticated uses. Exotic and rare are the dainty marionette figures fashioned by Richard Teschner in Vienna. From a performance of Javanese shadows witnessed in Munich the artist received the first suggestion for these delicate, precious creations. The thin, flexible limbs give us the feeling of the Eastern Wayangs. To this Teschner has gradually added a bit of the German folk spirit, quite noticeable in his society dramas where the little dolls resemble comfortable, bourgoisie Germans and only their fleshlessness reminds us of the Javanese origin. In other plays the Eastern flavor is purposely maintained. There is, for instance, the strange magician with the Assyrian headdress, or the enchantress in gorgeous stiff robes with menacing eyebrows, altogether oriental, and strange and beautiful. The grotesque and curiously misshapen animal forms conceived by Teschner remind us of deep-sea monsters similar to Hauptmann's Nickelmann and of early Christian conceptions of Infernal frightfulness to be found in the Witches' Kitchen of Faustus, or in the Temptations of St. Anthony. The smoothly finished, carefully fashioned naked figures have a rather brazen daintiness, permissible on the puppet stage alone. They offend perhaps at first sight by their deliberate daring but they possess a certain precise charm, a rather winning, rather quaint appeal. These precious little marionettes have been exhibited in private circles only.

In Baden-Baden just before the war a quite remarkable and thriving puppet show was to be found, belonging to Ivo Pühony. These clever dolls were carved out of wood and were most adroitly manipulated, marvellously so, we are told. The repertory of the puppets was very extensive and ambitious. At the outbreak of the war Ivo Pühony packed his dolls away in cases and left them in Baden-Baden. In 1914 Ernest Ehlert, actor and manager, and Fräulein E. Weissmann took the neglected little creatures to Berlin where they performed with tremendous success. They produced, among other things, *Doctor Sassafras*, a puppet play by Pocci and no less ambitious a drama than Goethe's *Faust*. The latter received a real ovation as a serious, artistic interpretation of the masterpiece; many witnesses declared the production more effective than when given upon the larger stage. The *Frankfürter Zeitung* contained this description of the performance: "The drama had a much purer and stronger emotional effect in this symbolic, miniature presentation with its modest and reliable lighting effects than is possible in the hard reality of the larger stage. The circle of the heavenly army shimmering in magic red reminding one of the pious fantasies of Beato Angelico; the voices of the archangels sounding from above; the gleam of white light when the voice of the Lord was heard; the dark chasm leading to the depths of the earth, out of which

MARIONETTES OF RICHARD TESCHNER, VIENNA
[Reproduced from *Deutsche Kunst und Dekoration*]

the wonderful little figure of Mephistopheles appeared and then, blinded by the radiance of Divinity, turned aside and covered himself with his bat's wing: all this provided a pure artistic satisfaction which called forth enthusiastic applause."

Less serious in nature but very remarkable were the famous *Two Dancing Chinamen* in the troupe of puppet actors. These agile little dolls, like figures from a Russian ballet, danced to the music of a phonograph with perfectly captivating antics. One witness has written: "It is hard to imagine how perfectly the slightly mechanical tone of the phonograph combines with the slightly mechanical motion of the figures to give an expression of what the fashionable philosopher of our day calls the *élan vital*." The last heard of Pühony's puppets was a prospective trip they were to take to the front for entertaining the soldiers and the grave problem of whether it would be wise to allow the erstwhile favorite marionette *Caruso* to go along, considering that, despite his power to amuse, he was after all a representative of the enemy.

Less excellent, crude puppet shows have gone wandering from village to village through Germany and Austria in recent years, but they have become more and more rare. These shows perform generally in the little town halls, with the villagers, high and low, crowding in to see performances of *Faust* (ever welcome) or Hamlet (with a happy ending), or, favorite of all, the life and death of the famous brigand *Schinder Hannes*. The love of the Germans for puppet entertainment is also constantly expressed in the little private puppet shows and shadow plays given by or for the children in their homes, usually gotten up for Christmas or birthday festivities.

In most Continental countries there may still be found traces and survivals of the old style puppet show and occasionally experiments with marionettes in the new manner. It is said that in Bohemia the marionette plays are the only form of drama now given in the native tongue. A very famous showman of Bohemia was Kopecki who travelled about with his show from town to town. A prominent Bohemian minister now residing in New York relates that he remembers these puppets and the terror which clutched his boyish heart whenever the little wooden devil appeared, opening and closing his horrible mouth and emitting the most inhuman and frightful noises. He remembers the comic characters of the shows, a rude peasant and his wife. The peasant always wielded a stick and there were many threatened beatings, but they never took place. In 1885 the names of Kopecki and of another showman, Winizki, were made doubly prominent by the publication of a book of their old puppet plays taken down in shorthand by two Viennese authors from performances they witnessed and written finally in wonderful Hoch-Deutsch.

In Hungary the gypsies have always been the puppeteers, travelling about with their rough little figures and accompaniment of music. From Mol-

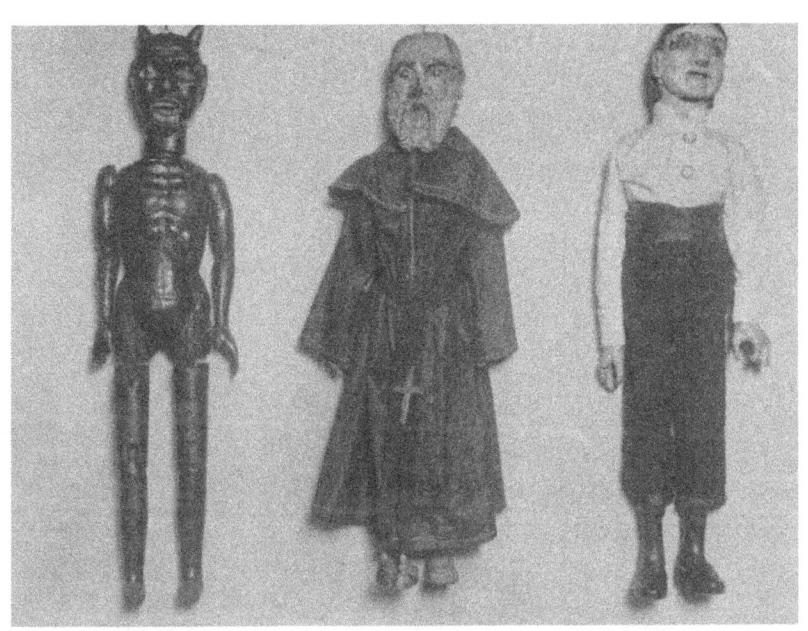

BOHEMIAN PUPPETS
Upper: Devil, Priest, Peasant
Lower: Soldier, King and Queen
[Property of the Reverend Vincent Pisek, New York]

MARIONETTES

davia comes a report of gypsy players at Christmas time in the olden days, one man crying out through the streets, "To the puppets, to the puppets!" followed by two other gypsies with a little theatre of marionettes. In these shows at the time of the Turkish wars in 1829 miniature Turks and Cossacks were made to belabor each other.

In Russia religious puppet plays were very common. There used to be in Moscow a regular mystery performed by marionettes on the Sunday before Christmas. It represented three Christian martyrs thrown into a fiery furnace and was performed in front of the great altar of the Moscow cathedral. Crude popular shows also wandered about and in 1812 Mr. Daniel Clarke discovered in Tartary, among the wandering Cossacks of the Don, common little dolls made to dance on a board by means of a string tied to the knees of a boy. These had probably been introduced and become established back in the remote ages in this out-of-the-way location.

Mr. Alexander Zelenko, formerly a professor at the University of Moscow, has written some interesting facts concerning modern Russian puppets. He says: "There still are travelling comedians who wander all over the country with their little outfits of dolls and folding screens. In most cases a so-called hand organ is used, and very often a monkey or a bird picks out the tickets of happiness. The performer uses a contrivance in his mouth to alter his voice for the different impersonations. The principal hero is 'Petrouchka' or 'Diminutive Peter,' the same as German 'Kasperle' and English 'Punch.' The hero makes much mischief in a horse trade with a gypsy or with a German doctor, a policeman or a recruiting officer. For such mischief the devil takes his body into hell.

"Even now, as in the olden times, satires on social endeavor are very often introduced, but only the common street-class enjoy them. From time to time the educators take part in this movement and try to raise the standard and to introduce the puppets into the school festivals.

"Some of these plays came into Russia from the West through Austria and Poland, — old Christmas beliefs connected with religious or nationalistic traditions. These Christmas Crib plays are mostly seen in Southern and Western Russia and Poland. Some of the Russian artists have been interested in the production and have given very fine performances. I myself introduced many of this kind of marionettes into the activities of the Children's Clubs in Moscow. Very interesting articles about the ethnographic and folklore value of these plays have been written in Russian scientific magazines."

In Poland, until the middle of the eighteenth century, there were frequent puppet performances given in churches and monasteries around Christmas time to amuse the people between mass and vespers. In the play of *Szopka* (stable) M. Magnin tells us there were little dolls of wood or cardboard representing

Mary, Jesus, Joseph, the angels, the shepherds, the three Magi on their knees with offerings of gold, incense and myrrh, not forgetting the ox and the ass and Saint John's lamb. There generally followed after this the massacre of the innocents in the midst of which Herod's own son perished by mistake. The wicked prince, in his despair, called upon Death who soon appeared in the form of a skeleton and cut off Herod's head with a scythe. Then a black devil with a red tongue, pointed horns and a long tail, ascended and picked up the King's body on his pitchfork and bore it off to perdition. To this peculiar performance were often added indecorous variations, despite the holy place in which it was performed. After being finally expelled from the interior of the churches, it continued to be popular for over a century, delighting both the rural and the urban population of Poland from Christmas to Shrove Tuesday. To this day performances of the Crib, or *Szopka*, are given by ambulant puppet shows. The text is sung and spoken: the figures, moving in pairs, represent characters of the old mysteries, also folk types, heroes, spirits, etc. The stage for these shows appears to be prescribed by tradition, of a certain structure, with intricate national architectural details. It is not surprising to learn that Stanislaw Wyspianski, Poland's great dramatic and poetic genius, was strongly interested in and influenced by this national type of puppet stage which seems to have been the original inspiration for his later strongly patriotic productions.

In Denmark, the puppets have pushed their way into literature. We find that Johan Ludvig Heiberg, a prominent Danish dramatist, has written several satirical marionette plays.

In Holland where *Jan-Classenspiel* have been long established, the puppet stage is a favorite diversion. Powel wrote in 1715 of its long standing popularity with the people and we are told that the cultured classes also found relaxation in the marionettes. Beyle states that during his studies at Rotterdam he always left his book at the sound of the showman's trumpet.

The little Polichinelle of Belgium is called *Woltje* which signifies little Walloon and he has many clownish but harmless tricks with which to delight his public. The popularity of the *Poechelnellespiel* in Brussels may be imagined from the fact that, prior to the war, there were fifteen standing puppet theatres offering every possible enticement. Two very famous showmen were Toone and Machieltje who for forty years gave performances to every class of audience, Machieltje specializing on the popular plays, Toone giving private performances. The successor of Toone was George Hembauf while the show of Machieltje descended to Laurent Broeders, who have a wonderfully equipped theatre in the suburbs. They possess over six hundred marionettes whose elegant costumes can be changed (there are over eleven hundred of these elaborate costumes). The Laurent Broeders do all the speaking for their dolls and the repertoire includes a wide range of subjects from important events in Flemish history to Dumas, adapted for puppets, and the old play of *Les Quatre Fils Aymon*. Another large puppet show is that of Pieter Buelens. He has four hundred puppets consisting chiefly of officers, chevaliers and kings, each knight so richly dressed that his robes cost from thirty to forty francs apiece. The dolls are about a metre high, made of cardboard and carefully articulated so that the gestures are extremely graceful. The scenery is naïve but picturesque; eight complete sets including two palace scenes, two wood scenes (one Winter, one Summer), two rooms, a prison, a rock, etc. The latest and most modern theatre for marionettes is the *Petit Théâtre* founded by a group of æsthetes, — Louis Picard, James Ensor, Thomas Braun, Gregoire le Roy, — and devoted to a naïvely refined art of puppetry. It was opened with the pastoral opera of Mozart, *Bastien et Bastienne*, the poetic version by Gautier-Villars.

In Antwerp the puppet shows are less elaborate and are generally to be found off in inconspicuous corners around the wharves where they are frequented chiefly by the laboring classes. There the drama varies from mockery of local occurrences to tales of Turks, bandits, kings, shepherds, sailors. One of these shows was the famous *Poesjenellenkelder*, the cave of the Polichinelles, where in a dark, gloomy cellar by the glimmer of a few smoking oil lamps the old and ever moving romantic dramas of the puppet show were performed for an appreciative and unspoiled audience. Hendrik Conscience, the Flemish novelist, has described how in his boyhood he often spent his last penny to witness the sufferings of the patient Genoveva or some similarly affecting performance. This old underground theatre, we are told, was open until the outbreak of the war.

Puppetry in England

> "Triumphant Punch! with joy I follow thee
> Through the glad progress of thy wanton course."

THUS exclaims Lord Byron, and he is but one of the long list of English poets, dramatists and essayists who have found delight and inspiration at the puppet booth. "One could hardly name a single poet from Chaucer to Byron, or a single prose writer from Sir Philip Sidney to Hazlitt in whose works are not to be found abundant information on the subject or frequent allusions to it. The dramatists, above all, beginning with those who are the glory of the reigns of Elizabeth and James I, supply us with the most curious particulars of the repertory, the managers, the stage of the marionettes." With this introduction M. Magnin brings forward a brilliant array of English authors in whose works we may find traces of the puppets, Shakespeare, Ben Jonson, Beaumont and Fletcher, Milton, Davenant, Swift, Addison, Steele, Gay, Fielding, Goldsmith, Sheridan and innumerable others.

In *The Winter's Tale* Autolycus remarks: "I know this man well. He hath been a process server, a bailiff, then he compassed a motion of *The Prodigal*

Son." Many other dramas of Shakespeare have similar allusions. Milton's *Areopagitica* contains these lines: "When God gave Adam reason, he gave him freedom to choose: he had else been a mere artificial Adam, such an Adam as seen in the motions."

Perhaps the casual mention of a popular diversion in the literature of a nation is not as impressive as the fact that it has served to suggest the themes of numberless dramas and poems. Shakespeare is said to have taken the idea for *Julius Cæsar* from the puppet play on the same subject which was performed near the Tower of London in his day; Ben Jonson's *Everyman Out of his Humour*, Robert Greene's *Orlando Furioso*, Dekker's best drolleries and certainly *Patient Grissel* in the composition of which he had a hand, Marlowe's *The Massacre at Paris* and many others may safely be said to have been suggested by the puppets. There are marionettes in Swift's *A Tale of a Tub*, illustrated by Hogarth.

Some authorities claim that Milton drew the argument for his great poem from an Italian marionette production of *Paradise Lost* which he once witnessed. Byron is supposed to have found the model for his *Don Juan* in the popular play of Punch's, *The Libertine Destroyed*. Hence it cannot be an exaggeration to state that even in England, where the puppets are not supposed to have attained such prestige as on the Continent, they were, nevertheless, not wholly insignificant nor without weight.

As is usually the case, the puppets in England

MARIONETTES

appear to have had a religious origin. Magnin mentions as an undoubted fact the movement of head and eyes on the Crucifix in the monastary of Boxley in Kent, and one hears not only of single articulated images but of passion plays performed by moving figures within the sacred edifices. E. K. Chambers has found the record of a Resurrection Play in the sixteenth century by "certain small puppets, representing the Persons of Christe, the Watchmen, Marie and others." This was at Whitney in Oxfordshire, "in the days of ceremonial religion," and one of these puppets which clacked was known as *Jack Snacker of Whitney*. It is certain that similar motions of sacred dramas and pageants given by mechanical statuettes were not unusual within the Catholic churches, and that during the reign of Henry VIII they were destroyed, as idols. Under Elizabeth and James, religious puppet-shows went wandering about the kingdom, giving the long drawn out moralities and mysteries, *The Prodigal Son, The Motion of Babylon* and *Nineveh with Jonah and the Whale*, a great favorite.

These early motions or drolls were a combination of dumb show, masques and even shadow play. Flögel explains that the masques were sometimes connected with the puppets or given sometimes as a separate play. "These masques," he writes, "consist of five tableaux or motions which take place behind a transparent curtain, just as in Chinese shadows. The showman, a silver-covered wand in his hand and a whistle for signalling, stands in front of the curtain and briefly informs the audience of the action of the piece. Thereupon he draws the curtain, names each personage by name as he appears, points out with his wand the various important actions of his actors' deeds, and relates the story more in detail than formerly. Another masque which Ben Jonson's *Bartholomew Fair* describes is quite different, for here the puppets themselves speak, that is, through a man hidden behind the scenes, who like the one standing out in front is called the interpreter."

As early as 1575 Italian pupazzi appeared in England and established themselves there. An order of the Lord Mayor of London at the time authorizes that, "Italian marionettes be allowed to settle in the city and to carry on their strange motions as in the past and from time immemorial." Piccini was a later Italian motion-man, but very famous, giving shows for fifty years and speaking for his *Punch* to the last with a foreign accent.

There is little doubt, despite much discussion, that the boisterous English Punch is a descendant of the puppet Pulcinello, brought over by travelling Italian showmen. Isaac d'Israeli writes of his ancestry, in the second volume of *Curiosities of Literature*, "Even Pullicinella, whom we familiarly call Punch, may receive like other personages of not greater importance, all his dignity from antiquity: one of his Roman ancestors having appeared to an antiquary's visionary eye in a bronze statue: more than one erudite dissertation authenticates the family likeness, the long nose, prominent and hooked; the goggle eyes; the hump at his back and breast; in a word all the character which so strongly marks the Punch race, as distinctly as whole dynasties have been featured by the Austrian lip or the Bourbon nose."

The origin of the name *Punch* has given rise to various theories. Some claim it is an anglicizing of Pulcinello, Pulchinello or Punchinello; others that it is derived as is Pulcinello from the Italian word *pulcino*, little chicken, either, some say, because of the squeak common to Punch and to the chicken or, others aver, because from little chicken might have come the expression for little boy, hence puppet. Again, it is maintained that the origin is the English provincialism *punch* (short, fat), allied to *Bunch*.

The older Punchinello was far less restricted in his actions and circumstances than his modern successor. He fought with allegorical figures representing want and weariness, as well as with his wife and the police. He was on intimate terms with the Patriarchs and the champions of Christendom, sat on the lap of the Queen of Sheba, had kings and lords for his associates, and cheated the Inquisition as well as the common hangman. After the revolution of 1688, with the coming of William and Mary, his prestige increased, and Mr. Punch took Mrs. Judy to wife and to them there came a child. The marionettes became more elaborate, were manipulated by wires and developed legs and feet. Queen Mary was often pleased to summon them into her palace. The young gallant, Punch, however, who had been but a garrulous roisterer, causing more noise than harm, began to develop into a merry but thick-skinned fellow, heretical, wicked, always victorious, overcoming Old Vice himself, the horned, tailed demon of the old English moralities. A modified Don Juan, when Don Juan was the vogue, he gradually became a vulgar pugnacious fellow to suit the taste of the lower classes.

During the reign of Queen Anne he was high in popular favor. *The Tatler* mentions him often, also *The Spectator;* Addison and Steele have both aided in immortalizing him. Famous showmen such as Mr. Powell included him in every puppet play, for what does an anachronism matter with the marionettes? He walked with King Solomon, entered into the affairs of Doctor Faustus, or the Duke of Lorraine or Saint George in which case he came upon the stage seated on the back of St. George's dragon to the delight of the spectators. One of his greatest successes was scored in *Don Juan or The Libertine Destroyed* where he was in his element, and we find him in the drama of Noah, poking his head from behind the side curtain while the floods were pouring down upon the Patriarch and his ark to remark, "Hazy weather, Mr. Noah." In one of Swift's satires, the popularity of Punch is declared to be so enormous that the audiences cared little for the plot of the play, merely waiting to greet the entrance of their beloved buffoon with shouts of laughter.

Punch hangs the Hangman
From a Cruikshank illustration of Payne-Collier's *Tragical Comedy of Punch and Judy*

At the beginning of the nineteenth century when Lord Nelson, as the hero of Abukir, was represented upon every puppet stage, he and Mr. Punch held the following dialogue:

"Come to my ship, my dear Punch, and help me defeat the French. If you like I will make you a Captain or a Commodore."

"Never, never," answered Punch. "I would not dare for I am afraid of being drowned in the deep sea."

"But don't have such absurd fears," replied the Admiral. "Remember that whoever is destined from birth to be hanged will never be drowned."

Gradually a sort of epic poem of Punch grew up, and there were regular scenes where the dissolute, hardened fellow beats his wife and child, defies morality and religion, knocks down the priest, fights the devil and overcomes him. In 1828 Mr. Payne-Collier arranged a series of little plays called *The Tragical Comedy of Punch and Judy*. In this labor he was assisted by the records of the Italian, Piccini, who, after long years of wandering through England, had established his Punch and Judy show in London. The series was profusely and delightfully illustrated by Cruikshank. These pictures and those of Hogarth have perpetuated for all times the funny features of Punch and Judy.

"With real conservatism," writes Maindron, "the English have preserved the figure and repertory of Punch almost as it was in the oldest days of Piccini and his predecessors." And it is thus one might find Punch on the street corner to-day, maltreating his long-suffering wife, teasing the dog, hanging the hangman. Mr. W. H. Pollock tells us of stopping with Robert Louis Stevenson to watch a Punch and Judy show given by a travelling showman in "bastard English and slang of the road." Stevenson delighted in it, and Mr. Pollock himself exclaimed: "Everybody who loves good, rattling melodrama with plenty of comic relief must surely love that great performance."

But to return to the shows and showmen of other times. In the Elizabethan period the motions were very prominent. The puppets sometimes took over plays of the day, and satirized them cleverly upon their own stages, the dolls costumed as nearly as possible like the prominent actors whom they imitated. Later, when for a time the Puritans abolished the theatres, the marionettes were allowed to continue their shows, and thus the entire repertory of the real stage fell into their hands. Permanent puppet stages grew up all over London: people thronged to the puppets.

In Ben Jonson's *Bartholomew Fair* he allows the showman, Lanthorn Leatherhead, to describe his fortunes: "Ah," he said, "I have made lots of money with *Sodom and Gomorrah* and with the *City of Norwich* but *Gunpowder Plot*, that was a veritable gift of God. It was that that made the pennies rain into the coffers. I only charged eighteen or twenty pence per head for admission, but I gave sometimes

MARIONETTES

nine or ten representations a day." Captain Pod, a seventeenth century showman mentioned in other writings of Ben Jonson, had a large repertory including, among other plays, *Man's Wit, Dialogue of Dives, Prodigal Son, Resurrection of the Saviour, Babylon, Jonah and the Whale, Sodom and Gomorrah, Destruction of Jerusalem, City of Nineveh, Rome and London, Destruction of Norwich, Massacre of Paris with the Death of the Duke de Guise* and *The Gunpowder Plot.* In 1667 Pepys records in his *Diary* that he found "my Lady Castlemane at a puppet play, Patient Grizell." *The Sorrows of Griselda*, indeed, was very popular at the time, also *Dick Whittington, The Vagaries of Merry Andrew* and *The Humours of Bartholomew Fair.* The marionettes, indeed, grew so much the vogue, and the rivalry was felt so keenly by the regular theatres, that in 1675 the proprietors of the theatre in Drury Lane and near Lincoln's Inn Fields formally petitioned that the puppets in close proximity be forbidden to exhibit, or be removed to a greater distance, as they interfered with the success of their performances.

But not alone the theatres objected to the competition of the puppets. One may read in *The Spectator, XVI,* that *young Mr. Powell* made his show a veritable thorn in the flesh of the clergy. It was stationed in Covent Garden, opposite the Cathedral of St. Paul, and Powell proceeded to use the church bell as a summons to his performances, luring away worshippers from the very door of the church. Finally the sexton was impelled to remonstrate. "I find my congregation taking the warning of my bell, morning and evening, to go to a puppet show set forth by one Powell, under the Piazzas, etc., etc. I desire you would lay this before the world, that Punchinello may choose an hour less canonical. As things are now, Mr. Powell has a full congregation while we have a very thin house."

This same Powell was the most successful motion maker of his day. He originated the *Universal Deluge* in which Noah and his family enter the ark, accompanied by all the animals, two and two. This show was given fifty-two consecutive nights, and was repeated two centuries later by the Prandi brothers in Florence. Powell had booths in London, Bath and Oxford, and played to most fashionable audiences. *The Tatler* and *The Spectator* mention him frequently. It was his Punch who sat on the Queen of Sheba's lap, who danced with Judy on the Ark, and made the famous remark to Noah concerning the weather. He gave numerous religious plays, such as the "Opera of Susannah or Innocence Betrayed, — which will be exhibited next week with a new pair of Elders." In 1713 he presented *Venus and Adonis or The Triumphs of Love*, a mock opera. As another attraction to his shows, the ingenious marionettist invented a fashion model, the little puppet, *Lady Jane*, who made a monthly appearance, bringing the latest styles from Paris. The ladies flocked to the puppets when she was announced on the bills.

A well known competitor of Powell was Pinkethman, in whose scenes the gods of Olympus ascended and descended to strains of music. Crawley was another rival. He advertised his show as follows: "At Crawley's Booth, over against the Crown Tavern in Smithfield, during the time of Bartholomew Fair, will be presented a little opera called the Old Creation of the World, yet newly revived, with addition of Noah's Flood, also several fountains, playing water during the time of the play. The last scene does present Noah and his family coming out of the Ark with all the beasts, two and two, and all the fowls of the air seen in a prospect sitting upon trees: likewise over the Ark is seen the sun rising in a glorious manner; moreover a multitude of angels will be seen in a double rank, which presents a double prospect, one for the sun, the other for the palace where will be seen six Angels ringing bells. Likewise Machines descend from above, double and treble, with Dives rising out of Hell and Lazarus seen in Abraham's bosom, besides several figures dancing jigs, sarabands, and country dances to the admiration of the spectators: with the merry conceits of Squire Punch and Sir John Spendall."

After these motion makers, came other showmen with many inventions. Colley Cibber wrote dramas for marionettes, and his daughter, the actress, Charlotte Clarke, founded a large puppet theatre. Russell, the old buffoon, is said to have been interested in this project also, but it finally failed. When the Scottish lords and other leaders of the Stuart uprising of 1745 were executed on Tower Hill, the beheading was made a feature by the puppet exhibitions at May Fair and was presented for many years after. Later Clapton's marionettes offered a play of Grace Darling rescuing the crew of the Forfarshire, "with many ingenious moving figures of quadrupeds." Boswell tells us in his *Life of Johnson* about Oliver Goldsmith, who was so vain he could not endure to have anyone do anything better than himself. "Once at an exhibition of the Fantoccini in London, when those who sat next to him observed with what dexterity a puppet was made to toss a pike, he could not bear that it should have such praise, and exclaimed with some warmth, 'Pshaw! I could do it better myself!' " Boswell adds in a note, "He went home with Mr. Burke to supper and broke his shin by attempting to exhibit to the company how much better he could jump over a stick than the puppets." Dr. Johnson was a great admirer of the fantoccini in London, and considered a performance of *Macbeth* by puppets as satisfactory as when played by human actors.

At the end of the eighteenth century, Flockton's show displayed five hundred figures at work in various trades. Browne's *Theatre of Arts*, 1830-1840 travelled about at country fairs showing *The Battle of Trafalgar, Napoleon's Army Crossing the Alps* and the *Marble Palace of St. Petersburg*. Some marionettes of the nineteenth century became satirical, attacking literature and politics with mischievous

MARIONETTES

energy. Punch assumed a thousand disguises; he caricatured Sheridan, Fox, Lord Nelson. William Hazlitt wrote seriously in praise of puppet shows. There are gaps in the history of English puppets which seem to imply a decline in the popularity of that amusement. One comes upon occasional records of shows straggling through the countryside, and giving the old, timeworn productions of *Prodigal Son* or *Noah*, or *Pull Devil, Pull Baker*. During the reign of George IV, puppets were found at street corners, dancing sailors, milkmaids, clowns, but Punch, as ever, the favorite.

Even now, puppets on boards may be seen in the streets of London. Of the old shows, one resident of that city relates: "When I was a child, marionettes used to go about the streets of London in a theatre on wheels about as big as a barrel organ, but I dare say I am wrong about size, because one cannot remember these things. I remember particularly a skeleton which danced and came to pieces so that his bones lay about in a heap. When I was properly surprised at this he assembled himself and danced again. I was so young that I was rather frightened."

There is to-day one of the old professional marionette showmen wandering about in England, Clunn Lewiss, who still has a set of genuine old dolls, bought up from a predecessor's outfit. For fifty years he has been traveling along the roads, like a character strayed out of Dickens. He has interested members of artistic coteries in London, who have been moved by the old man's appeals for help, and some attempts have been made to revive interest in his show. Surely Clunn Lewiss deserves some recognition.

Altogether unconnected with popular puppets were the highly complicated mechanical exhibitions of Holden's marionettes. The amazing feats performed by Holden's puppets astonished not only England, but all the large Continental and American cities where they were displayed. They were tremendously admired. The surprising dexterity of manipulation, and the elegance of the settings had never been surpassed. In Paris, however, de Goncourt wrote of them: "The marionettes of Holden! These creatures of wood are a little disquieting. There is a dancer turning on the tips of her toes in the moonlight that might be a character of Hoffman, etc.

"Holden was more of an illusionist than a true marionettist. He produced exact illusions of living beings, but he was lacking in imagination. The fantoches of Holden were certainly marvels of precision, but they appeal to the eye and not to the spirit. One admired, one did not laugh at them. They astonished, but they did not charm."

There have been several interesting amateur marionette shows within the last decade. There are the Wilkinsons, two clever modern painters who have taken their puppets from village to village in England and also in France. They traveled about with their family in a caravan and wherever they wished to

OLD ENGLISH PUPPETS
Used by Mr. Clunn Lewiss in his wandering show
[Courtesy of Mr. Tony Sarg]

MARIONETTES

give a show, they halted and drew forth a stage from the rear end of the wagon. Their dolls are eight inches high or more and they require four operators. They are designed with a touch of caricature, and they perform little plays and scenes invented by the Wilkinsons, very amusing and witty. Not long ago Mr. Gair Wilkinson gave a very successful exhibition of his show at the Margaret Morris Theater in Chelsea for a short season.

The Ilkely Players, of Ilkely, Yorkshire, are a group of young women who produced puppet plays for some five or six years, touring through England. Their dolls were rather simple, mechanically; only the arms were articulated, for the most part; the heads were porcelain dolls' heads. Nevertheless this group of puppeteers deserves the credit they attained by reviving the classic old show of *Doctor Faustus*, at Clifford's Inn Hall, Chelsea. They also gave very interesting productions of Maeterlinck's *The Seven Princesses*, and Thackeray's *The Rose and the Ring*, dramatized by Miss Dora Nussey, who was the leader of the group. Inspired by their success, Miss Margaret Bulley of Liverpool produced a puppet play of Faustus before the Sandon Studio Club. Miss Bulley's puppets were quite simple wooden dolls with papier-maché heads and tin arms and legs, each worked with seven black threads. The costumes were copied after old German engravings of the eighteenth century and the production proved very effective.

Most highly perfected, and most exquisite of English puppets to-day, are those of the artist, Mr. William Simmonds, in Hampstead. They originated in a village in Wiltshire as an amusement at a Christmas party given by Mr. and Mrs. Simmonds every year to the village children. The audience was so delighted that the next year more puppets were made with a more attractive setting. Friends then became so enthusiastic that the creators of the puppets realized what might be done, and in London, the following Spring, they began giving small private shows.

The productions are only suited to a small audience of forty or fifty. The puppets are mostly fifteen inches high, some smaller; the stage is nine feet wide, six deep, and a little over two feet high. The scenery is painted on small screens. At present there are three scenes, a Harlequinade, a Woodland Scene and a little Seaport Town. The puppets are grouped to use one or the other of these scenes. They do not do plays but seem to find their best expression in songs and dances connected with various by-play and "business" and a slight thread of episode which is often varied, never twice alike. Mr. Simmonds manipulates the puppets entirely alone and cannot work with anyone close. He frequently operates a puppet in each hand, all with the utmost dexterity and delicacy, and manages others by means of hanging them up and moving them slightly at intervals, at the same time singing, whistling, improvising dialogue or imitating various noises! People gener-

Mr. Gair Wilkinson and Assistant at Work on the Bridge of their Puppet Theatre
[Reproduced from *The Sketch*, 1916]

ally expect to find half a dozen manipulators behind the scenes.

Mr. Simmonds himself carves the heads, hands and feet of his marionettes in wood (usually lime) and paints them in tempera to avoid shine. They are beautifully done. Some are dressed, some have clothes painted on them. Some are quite decorative, others impressionistic or frankly realistic. Not contented with the little-bit-clumsy doll, Mr. Simmonds has perfected his puppets with great technical skill until they move with perfect naturalness, some with dignity, some with grace, some with humor, each according to its nature.

In the Harliquinade the scene is hung with black velvet, lighted from the front, which gives the effect of a black void against which the figures of Harlequin, Columbine, Clown, Pantaloon and others appear with sparkling brilliancy and vivid color. In the Seaport Town, a medley of characters appear, — a sailor, a grenadier, a fat woman, an old man, the minister, etc. There are songs used in this to give variety. Particularly clever is an English sailor of the time of Nelson who comes out of a public house and dances a jig, heel-tapping the floor in perfect time, his hands on his hips and his body rollicking in perfect character while he sings, "On Friday morn when we set sail." Another excellent dancing doll is the washerwoman of the old sort, short and stout and great-armed, jolly and roughfaced.

In the Woodland Scene, creatures of the wood

appear, — faun, dryad, nymph, young centaurs, baby faun, hunted stag, a forester, a dainty shepherd and a shepherdess, etc. The little sketch is entirely wordless, having only musical accompaniment played by Mrs. Simmonds upon a virginal or a spinet, or an early Erard piano (date 1804). The sound is just right in scale for the puppets; anything else would seem heavy. The fauns in this scene are most popular, particularly the *Baby* who has an extraordinary tenderness, and skips and leaps with the agility of a live thing. The act of extreme dreaminess and beauty is described thus by one who was privileged to witness it. "In one scene a man went out hunting. He hid behind a bush. A stag came on. He shot the stag which lay down and died. Then there came one or two creatures of the wood, who could do nothing, and at last a very beautiful nymph, lightly clothed in leaves. She succeeded in resuscitating the stag, who got up and bounded away. When they had gone, the hunter who had watched it all from behind the bush came out, and that was all. Music all the time. No words. The stag was quite astonishing."

Although he is now living and working in Florence, Mr. Gordon Craig must not be omitted from any account of English marionettes and advocates of the puppets. Quite apart from the class of artistic amateurs and equally remote from the usual professional marionettist of to-day, Mr. Craig stands rather as a new prophet of puppetry, recalling in stirring terms

MARIONETTES

the virtues of the old art, and adding his new and individual interpretation of its value.

Puppets are but a small portion of the dramatic experiment and propaganda which Mr. Craig is so courageously carrying on in Florence. But they are not the least interesting branch of his undertakings. He has assembled a veritable museum of marionette and shadow play material from all over the world. Pictures of some parts of his collection appear regularly in "The Marionette." There are also delightful puppet plays appearing in this pamphlet. But this is not all.

With the marionette used as a sort of symbol, Mr. Craig has been conducting research into the very heart of dramatic verities, and producing dramatic formulas which should apply on any stage at any time. He has invented his marionettes to express dramatic qualities which he deems significant, and in his puppets he has attempted to eliminate all other disturbing and unnecessary qualities. Thus he creates little wooden patterns or models for his artists of the stage, and he applies in actual usage Goethe's maxim: "He who would work for the stage . . . should leave nature in her proper place and take careful heed not to have recourse to anything but what may be performed by children with puppets upon boards and laths, together with sheets of cardboard and linen."

At the beginning of his experiments with marionettes Mr. Craig and his assistants constructed one large and extremely complicated doll which was moved on grooves and manipulated by pedals from below, with a small *telltale* to indicate to the operator the exact effect produced. But this marionette was not satisfactory for Mr. Craig's purposes.

He then directed his energies in an exactly opposite direction, toward simplification. The result was small, but very impressive dolls, carved out of wood and painted in neutral colors, — the color of the scenes in which they moved, to allow for the fullest and most variable effects produced by lighting. Most interesting, too, the manner in which Mr. Craig applied his theories concerning gesture with these little puppets. Each marionette was allowed to make one or two gestures, — no more. But these gestures had to be exact, invariable, and the perfect indication of whatever meaning they were intended to convey. Before inventing the action of a puppet, Mr. Craig would study, for days or weeks, watching various people making the movement and expressing the emotion he desired to portray. Then he would extract from these observations the general and essential qualities of this particular gesture; all else, due to the peculiarities of individuals, was left out as irrelevant for the stage. Hence when Mr. Craig's puppet moves, it moves simply, significantly and — one more essential — surely. For nothing is left to chance. The gesture, once selected, is produced with infinite care and is made invariable. No whim of the manipulator, no accident of chance, can alter it.

MARIONETTES

One motion of the finger operates the figure, and the result is assured.

Naturally a character may be required to exhibit varied succeeding emotions, not encompassed by one or two motions. In that case the figure is taken off the stage and replaced by another similar in appearance but differently articulated for a different purpose. There are sometimes as many as six or eight puppets for one character. Mr. Craig has experimented with his marionettes in many plays, some comedy, some tragedy. It is not recorded whether he has ever given one finished puppet production: it is immaterial. The idea embodied in these little puppets is immense, — a valuable and lasting contribution to constructive dramatic criticism.

The Marionettes in America

> "They come from far away. They have been the joy of innumerable generations which preceded our own; they have gained, with our direct ancestors, many brilliant successes; they have made them laugh but they have also made them think; they have had eminent protectors; for them celebrated authors have written. At all times they have enjoyed a liberty of manners and language which has rendered them dear to the people for whom they were made."
>
> ERNEST MAINDRON

How old are the marionettes in America? How old indeed! Older than the white races which now inhabit the continent, ancient as the ancient ceremonials of the dispossessed native Indians, more indigenous to the soil than we who prate of them, — such are the first American marionettes!

Dramatic ceremonials among the Indians are numerous, even at the present time. Each tribe has its peculiar, individual rites, performed, as a rule, by members of the tribe dressed in prescribed, symbolic costumes and wearing often a conventionalized mask. Occasionally, however, articulated figures take part in these performances along with the human participants. Dr. Jesse Walter Fewkes has published a minute description of a theatrical performance

MARIONETTES

at Walpi which he witnessed in 1900, together with pictures of the weird and curious snake effigies employed in it.

The Great Serpent drama of the Hopi Indians, called *Palü lakonti*, occurs annually in the March moon. It is an elaborate festival, the paraphernalia for which are repaired or manufactured anew for days preceding the event. There are about six acts and while one of them is being performed in one room, simultaneously shows are being enacted in the other eight *kivas* on the East Mesa. The six sets of actors pass from one room to another, in all of which spectators await their coming. Thus, upon one night each performance was given nine times and was witnessed by approximately five hundred people. The drama lasts from nine P.M. until midnight.

Dr. Fewkes gives us the following description of the first act: "A voice was heard at the hatchway, as if some one were hooting outside, and a moment later a ball of meal, thrown into the room from without, landed on the floor by the fireplace. This was a signal that the first group of actors had arrived, and to this announcement the fire tenders responded, 'Yunya ai,' 'Come in,' an invitation which was repeated by several of the spectators. After considerable hesitation on the part of the visitors, and renewed cries to enter from those in the room, there was a movement above, and the hatchway was darkened by the form of a man descending. The fire tenders arose, and held their blankets about the fire to darken the room. Immediately there came down the ladder a procession of masked men bearing long poles upon which was rolled a cloth screen, while under their blankets certain objects were concealed. Filing to the unoccupied end of the kiva, they rapidly set up the objects they bore. When they were ready a signal was given, and the fire tenders, dropping their blankets, resumed their seats by the fireplace. On the floor before our astonished eyes we saw a miniature field of corn, made of small clay pedestals out of which projected corn sprouts a few inches high. Behind this field of corn hung a decorated cloth screen reaching from one wall of the room to the other and from the floor almost to the rafters. On this screen were painted many strange devices, among which were pictures of human beings, male and female, and of birds, symbols of rain-clouds, lightning, and falling rain. Prominent among the symbols was a row of six circular disks the borders of which were made of plaited corn husks, while the enclosed field of each was decorated with a symbolic picture of the sun. Men wearing grotesque masks and ceremonial kilts stood on each side of this screen.

"The act began with a song to which the masked men, except the last mentioned, danced. A hoarse roar made by a concealed actor blowing through an empty gourd resounded from behind the screen, and immediately the circular disks swung open upward, and were seen to be flaps, hinged above, covering orifices through which simultaneously protruded

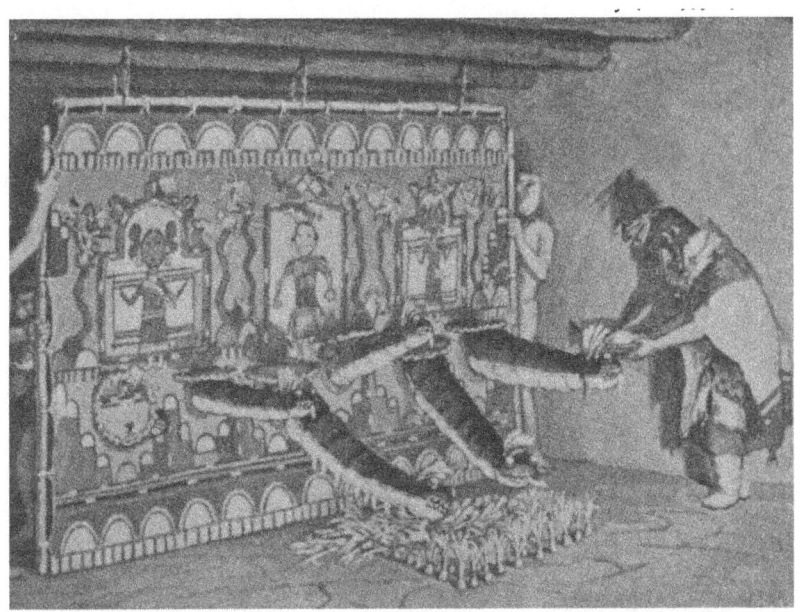

MARIONETTES EMPLOYED IN CEREMONIAL DRAMA OF THE AMERICAN INDIANS
Upper: Serpent effigies, screen and miniature corn field used in Act I of the *Great Serpent Drama* of the Hopi Katcinas
[From *A Theatrical Performance at Walpi*, by J. Walter Fewkes, in the Proceedings of the Washington Academy of Sciences, 1900, Vol. II]
Lower: Drawing by a Hopi Indian of articulated figurines of corn maidens and birds
[From *Hopi Katcinas*, by J. Walter Fewkes]

six artificial heads of serpents, realistically painted. Each head had protuberant goggle eyes, and bore a curved horn and a fan-like crest of hawk feathers. A mouth with teeth was cut in one end, and from this orifice there hung a strip of leather, painted red, representing the tongue.

"Slowly at first, but afterwards more rapidly, these effigies were thrust farther into view, each revealing a body four or five feet long, painted, like the head, black on the back and white on the belly. When they were fully extended the song grew louder, and the effigies moved back and forth, raising and depressing their heads in time, wagging them to one side or the other in unison. They seemed to bite ferociously at each other, and viciously darted at men standing near the screen. This remarkable play continued for some time, when suddenly the heads of the serpents bent down to the floor and swept across the imitation corn field, knocking over the clay pedestals and the corn leaves which they supported. Then the effigies raised their heads and wagged them back and forth as before. It was observed that the largest effigy, or that in the middle, had several udders on each side of the belly, and that she apparently suckled the others. Meanwhile the roar emitted from behind the screen by a concealed man continued, and wild excitement seemed to prevail. Some of the spectators threw meal at the effigies, offering prayers, amid shouts from others. The masked man, representing a woman, stepped forward and presented the contents of the basket tray to the serpent effigies for food, after which he held his breasts to them as if to suckle them.

"Shortly after this the song diminished in volume, the effigies were slowly drawn back through the openings, the flaps on which the sun symbols were painted fell back in place, and after one final roar, made by the man behind the screen, the room was again silent. The overturned pedestals with their corn leaves were distributed among the spectators, and the two men by the fireplace again held up their blankets before the fire, while the screen was silently rolled up, and the actors with their paraphernalia departed."

There are some acts in the drama into which the serpent effigies do not enter at all. In the fifth act these Great Snakes rise up out of the orifices of two vases instead of darting out from the screen. This action is produced by strings hidden in the kiva rafters, the winding of heads and struggles and gyrations of the sinuous bodies being the more realistic because in the dim light the strings were invisible.

In the fourth act two masked girls, elaborately dressed in white ceremonial blankets, usually participate. Upon their entrance they assume a kneeling posture and at a given signal proceed to grind meal upon mealing stones placed before the fire, singing, and accompanied by the clapping of hands. "In some years marionettes representing Corn Maids are substituted for the two masked girls," Dr. Fewkes explains, "in the act of grinding corn, and these two figures are very skillfully manipulated by concealed actors. Although this representation was not introduced in 1900, it has often been described to me, and one of the Hopi men has drawn me a picture of the marionettes."

"The figurines are brought into the darkened room wrapped in blankets, and are set up near the middle of the kiva in much the same way as the screens. The kneeling images, surrounded by a wooden framework, are manipulated by concealed men; when the song begins they are made to bend their bodies backward and forward in time, grinding the meal on miniature metates before them. The movements of girls in grinding meal are so cleverly imitated that the figurines moved by hidden strings at times raised their hands to their faces, which they rubbed with meal as the girls do when using the grinding stones in their rooms.

"As this marionette performance was occurring, two bird effigies were made to walk back and forth along the upper horizontal bar of the framework, while bird calls issued from the rear of the room."

The symbolism of this drama is intricate and curious. The effigies representing the Great Serpent, an important supernatural personage in the legends of the Hopi Indians, are somehow associated with the Hopi version of a flood; for it was said that when the ancestors of certain clans lived far south this monster once rose through the middle of the pueblo plaza, drawing after him a great flood which submerged the land and which obliged the Hopi to migrate into his present home, farther North. The snake effigies knocking over the cornfields symbolize floods, possible winds which the Serpent brings. The figureines of the Corn Maids represent the mythical maidens whose beneficent gift of corn and other seeds, in ancient times, is a constant theme in Hopi legends.

The effigies which Dr. Fewkes saw used were not very ancient, but in olden times similar effigies existed and were kept in stone enclosures outside the pueblos. The house of the *Ancient Plumed Snake of Hano* is in a small cave in the side of a mesa near the ruins of Turkinobi where several broken serpent heads and effigy ribs (or wooden hoops) can now be seen, although the entrance is walled up and rarely used.

The puppet shows commonly seen to-day in the United States are of foreign extraction or at least inspired by foreign models. For many years there have been puppet-plays throughout the country. Visiting exhibitions like those of Holden's marionettes which Professor Brander Matthews praises so glowingly are, naturally, rare. But one hears of many puppets in days past that have left their impression upon the childhood memories of our elders, travelling as far South as Savannah or wandering through the New England states. Our vaudevilles and sideshows and galleries often have exhibits of mechanical dolls, such as the amazing feats of *Mantell's Marionette Hippodrome Fairy-land Transformation* which advertises "Big scenic novelty, seventeen

MARIONETTES

gorgeous drop curtains, forty-five elegant talking acting figures in a comical pantomime," or *Madam Jewel's Manikins* in Keith's Circuit, Madam Jewel being an aunt of Holden, they say, and guarding zealously with canvas screens the secret of her devices, even as Holden himself is said to have done.

Interesting, too, is the story of the retired marionettist, Harry Deaves, who writes: "I have on hand forty to fifty marionette figures, all in fine shape and dressed. I have been in the manikin business forty-five years, played all the large cities from coast to coast, over and over, always with big success; twenty-eight weeks in Chicago without a break with Uncle Tom's Cabin, a big hit. The reason I am selling my outfit is, — I am over sixty years of age and I don't think I will work it again." How one wishes one might have seen that *Uncle Tom's Cabin* in Chicago! In New York at present there is Remo Buffano, reviving interest in the puppets by giving performances now and then in a semi-professional way with large, simple dolls resembling somewhat the Sicilian burattini. His are plays of adventure and fairy lore.

Then, too, in most of our larger cities from time to time crude popular shows from abroad are to be found around the foreign neighborhoods. It is said that at one time in Chicago there were Turkish shadow plays in the Greek Colony; Punch and Judy make their appearance at intervals, and Italian or Sicilian showmen frequently give dramatic versions of the legends of Charlemagne.

In Cleveland two years ago a party of inquisitive folk went one night to the Italian neighborhood in search of such a performance. We found and entered a dark little hall where the rows of seats were crowded closely together and packed with a spellbound audience of Italian workingmen and boys. Squeezing into our places with as little commotion as possible we settled down to succumb to the spell of the crude foreign fantoccini, large and completely armed, who were violently whacking and slashing each other before a rather tattered drop curtain. Interpreted into incorrect English by a small boy glued to my side, broken bits of the resounding tale of *Orlando Furioso* were hissed into my ear. But for these slangy ejaculations one might well have been in the heart of Palermo. A similar performance is described by Mr. Arthur Gleason. It was a show in New York, the master of which was Salvatore Cascio, and he was assisted by Maria Grasso, daughter of the Sicilian actor, Giovanni Grasso of Catania.

"For two hours every evening for fifty evenings the legends unrolled themselves, princes of the blood and ugly unbelievers perpetually warring." There was, explains Mr. Gleason, some splendid fighting. "Christians and Saracens generally proceeded to quarrel at close range with short stabbing motions at the opponent's face and lungs. After three minutes they swing back and then clash!! sword shivers on shield!! Three times they clash horridly, three times retire to the wings, at last the Christian beats down

ITALIAN MARIONETTE SHOW
Operated in Cleveland for a season. Proprietor, Joseph Scionte
[Courtesy of Cleveland *Plain Dealer*]

MARIONETTES

his foe; the pianist meanwhile is playing violent ragtime during the fight, five hidden manipulators are stamping on the platform above, the cluttered dead are heaped high on the stage." When one considers that such puppets are generally about three feet high and weigh one hundred pounds, armor and all, and are operated by one or two thick iron rods firmly attached to the head and hands, what wonder that the flooring of the stage is badly damaged by the terrific battles waged upon it and has to be renewed every two weeks!

Far removed from these unsophisticated performances, however, are the poetic puppets of the Chicago Little Theatre. I use the present tense optimistically despite the sad fact that the Little Theatre in Chicago has been closed owing to unfavorable conditions caused by the war. But although "Puck is at present cosily asleep in his box," as Mrs. Maurice Browne has written, we all hope that the puppets so auspiciously successful for three years will resume their delightful activities, somehow or other, soon.

At first the originators of the Chicago marionettes travelled far into Italy and Germany, seeking models for their project. Finally in Solln near Munich they discovered Marie Janssen and her sister, whose delicate and fantastic puppet plays most nearly approached their own ideals. They brought back to Chicago a queer little model purchased in Munich from the man who had made Papa Schmidt's Puppen. But, as one of the group has written, the little German puppet seemed graceless under these skies. And so, Ellen Van Volkenburg (Mrs. Maurice Browne) and Mrs. Seymour Edgerton proceeded to construct their own marionettes. Miss Katherine Wheeler, a young English sculptor, modelled the faces, each a clear-cut mask to fit the character, but left purposely rough in finish. Miss Wheeler felt that the broken surfaces carried the facial expression farther. The puppets were fourteen inches high, carved in wood. The intricate mechanism devised by Harriet Edgerton rendered the figures extremely pliable. Her mermaids, with their serpentine jointing, displayed an uncanny sinuousness. Miss Lillian Owen was Mistress of the Needle, devising the filmy costumes, and Mrs. Browne with fine technique and keen dramatic sense took upon herself the task of training and inspiring the puppeteers as well as creating the poetic ensemble.

The Chicago puppets are neither grotesque nor humorous and they have little in common with the puppet of tradition. Theirs is an element of exquisite magical fairy-land, with dainty beings moving about in it, who can express beauty, tragedy and tenderness. Their repertoire consists for the most part of fantasies written or adapted by members of the group. The first was a delicious fairy adventure, a play for children, *The Deluded Dragon*, founded upon an old Chinese legend, wherein a lovely Prince seems to follow a Wooden Spoon down the River certain that he will chance upon Adventure, which

MARIONETTES AT THE CHICAGO LITTLE THEATRE
Production of *Alice in Wonderland* under Mrs. Maurice Browne's direction
Upper: The Duchess's Kitchen
Lower: The White Rabbit's House

he does. The play was decidedly successful, despite a most unfortunate accident at the first performance caused by the impetuosity of the somewhat hurried puppeteers. To be more explicit, "the fierce but fragile dragon parted in the middle, his five heads swinging free of his timorously lashing tail." "The same year," continues Miss Hettie Louise Mick, herself puppeteer and composer of marionette plays, "Reginald Arkell's charming fantasy, *Columbine*, was produced with more patience and proved a wholly delightful and almost finished thing."

The next year two fairy tales were presented, *Jack and the Beanstalk* and *The Little Mermaid*, both dramatized by the puppeteers. Great technical advances had been made in the latter play and a delicate, fantastic effect attained, approaching the ideals of the founders. The last and most ambitious performance of this season was Shakespeare's *A Midsummer Night's Dream*, given not only for children but openly for the grown-ups. Of this production Miss Mick has written: "Puck, who had been known formerly as the rather stiff little fairy who introduced and closed each play in rhyme, now became his romping, pliant self, tumbling through the air, doubling up in chortling glee upon his toadstool and pushing his annoying little person into every disconcerted mortal's way. Titania emerged, a glowing queen of filmy draperies, attended by flitting elves, and Oberon resumed his crafty, flashing earth-character, his attendants being two inflated and wholly impudent bugs. The Mechanicals, while clumsy, fulfilled their parts well and brought the outworn humor of Shakespeare into hilarious reality, the scene between Pyramus and Thisbe never failing to bring roars of appreciation from the audience. Only the Greeks were a dank and dismal failure. Hurriedly constructed to meet the rapidly approaching production date, they were awkward, long-headed, stiff-jointed creatures highly unlike their graceful originals. But the lighting and settings, and the prevailing atmosphere of exquisite unreality were such that the audience came night after night for five weeks, and at the end of that time, when the theatre closed for the season, demanded more."

Mrs. Browne, in an informal letter about her puppets, has written concerning this performance: "I don't think I ever have seen such delicate beauty as was achieved at the end of the Midsummer: I say it in all simplicity because I have a curious, Irish feeling that the little dolls took matters into their own hands and for once allowed us a glimpse into their own secret world. The audience, whether of adults or of children, never failed to respond with a sudden hush and the poor, tired girls who had been working in great heat over the colored lights for two hours never failed to get their reward." Mrs. Browne then proceeded to give an idea of the patient toil behind the scenes. "We rehearsed six hours a day for about seven weeks to prepare the play. Six girls worked the puppets; there were about thirty of them, so you can see how many characters each girl had to create and how many dolls she had to work (my puppeteers spoke for each puppet they handled). Besides the actual workers, I had an understudy whose duty it was to stand on the platform back of the girls to take their puppets from them when the scenes were moving quickly and many characters were leaving the stage at once; she then hung the puppets where they could be easily reached for their next entrance. Hers was, of course, the most thankless task of all because she had none of the pleasure, and the accuracy of the performance depended upon her efficiency. None who have not worked with puppets can understand the nervous strain of these performances."

The third year of the Chicago puppets saw progress in many directions. The enthusiasm of the puppeteers had finally been aroused to the point where each contributed suggestions in the line of mechanical construction or the adapting of plays. Mr. H. Carrol French of the South Bend Little Theatre came to be puppet manager and added many improvements to the mechanism of the dolls, constructing the bodies of wire instead of wood (some suggestions for which he received through the courtesy of Mr. Tony Sarg). The new dolls were more sensitive to manipulation than the old, and more individual in their gestures. The repertoire for this season consisted of two little fairy plays, *The Frog Prince* and *Little Red Riding Hood*, adaptations of Miss Mick, and then *Alice in Wonderland,* made into a play by Mrs. Browne. While this play never wove so strong a poetic spell as *A Midsummer Night's Dream,* it marked great strides in skill on the part of the manipulators. This same year the little puppets went on a tour, not only into the suburbs of Chicago but, under the auspices of the Drama League, as far as St. Louis. Let us hope that at some not too distant date Puck, moving sprite among this brave and poetic band of marionettes, will gaily revive and travel farther with his troupe so that we all may witness and enjoy his fairy charms.[1]

The Cleveland Playhouse has had its puppet stage from the very beginning of the organization. Mr. Raymond O'Neil, the director, has always taken a great interest in the puppets. He believes, with Mr. Gordon Craig, that they might well serve as models in style, simplicity and impersonality for living actors, but he also avers that they are capable of presenting certain types of drama as effectively if not more satisfactorily than the best of actors, and certainly better than any second-rate performers. When the Cleveland Playhouse was still a very small, informal group it was decided to produce a serious marionette play. The director selected for this pur-

[1] Mrs. Browne, in any case, has not been discouraged. In 1918 she instructed her class in the dramatic department of the University of Utah in the principles and methods of marionette play, developing possible puppeteers for the future. The next spring we find her assisting Mr. Sarg in directing and staging his little puppet drama, *The Rose and the Ring.*

MARIONETTES AT THE CLEVELAND PLAY HOUSE
Presenting *The Life of Chopin*
Puppets and scenery designed by Carl Broemel

pose *The Death of Tintagiles*, written by Maeterlinck expressely for puppets. A Cleveland artist, Mr. George Clisby, worked out the proper proportions for the marionettes and the stage and their relation to each other. It is recognized by all who witness them that the effectiveness and success of the Cleveland productions are due in great part to the happy proportions prevailing in the marionette scenes and the sense of a complete, harmonious whole which they create.

Mr. Clisby also designed the costumes for the first dolls, and the scenery. Only the significant and essential was allowed upon his little stage, strong, simple lines and colors, a few poplar trees upon a hilltop in the blue dusk of the evening, or plain, gloomy chambers with high arches leading away into mysterious passages, or at the very last, merely a door, a massive, closed iron door set in bare walls. The figures were planned in the same spirit. Being very small they were given practically no features, a scowling eyebrow, a dignified beard, long hair or short, stiff or flowing, being sufficient indication of the type represented.

Miss Grace Treat, who made and dressed most of the marionettes, caught and embodied the artist's ideal in strange, tall puppets, naïve but marvelously impressive. The construction of these puppets, although extremely simple, had to be planned and executed patiently. Often a marionette was taken apart and made over again until the right effect, or the proper gesture, was obtained. The puppets are somewhat like rag dolls, of a soft material, stuffed with cotton or scraps, weighted and carefully balanced with lead. Five and at most seven strings are used and the control is very primitive. This studied simplicity in structure and in costume has given the Cleveland puppets a naïve style, — their limitations both defining and emphasizing the significance of each little figure. Miss Treat was also the master-manipulator of the puppets and in her hands the stiff little Ygraine took on heroic and tragic proportions.

For many months a small group of faithful enthusiasts struggled to attain the standard set for them by director and artist. The play was finally given before an audience of Playhouse members. Mr. O'Neil produced the strangely beautiful lighting with the crudest facilities imaginable. The parts were read by members of the group who had been working along patiently with the manipulators until words, settings and action had grown perfectly harmonious. Those who were privileged to witness this first production were deeply thrilled by the poetic beauty of it, and still mention it as an unusual experience.

Encouraged by this initial success, the group determined to continue with marionettes. But the Playhouse itself was going through a winter of vicissitudes and the puppeteers were compelled to endure and suffer many delays and disappointments. Rehearsing in a rear room of an empty house loaned for the season (and often fabulously cold!) with readers

MARIONETTES

and operators dropping out one by one from sheer discouragement or because of war work, trying out several plays which for one reason or another proved impossible, still a nucleus of the old group, with the addition of á few new workers, held on, held out through this second season under the ever optimistic leadership of Grace Treat. After moving into other temporary quarters, to be exact, into the high and dingy little ball-room of an old residence turned boarding-house, the group produced a very successful repetition of *Tintagiles*.[1]

Meanwhile the Playhouse had purchased a little church which it remodeled, decorated and equipped as a permanent theatre. During this time, and under most trying circumstances brought about by the war, the director contrived to present several productions for the first Winter in the new playhouse, among them two marionette performances. Most of the puppeteers and readers for both of these plays were new at the work and had to be trained from the very beginning. The stage, too, had been altered to admit of a cyclorama, improved lighting arrangements and, quite incidentally, a stronger and safer *bridge*. Nevertheless certain methods and principles of manipulating were evolved which somewhat raised the dexterity of the group as a whole.

[1] At the same time a less successful and quite unfinished dress rehearsal of another drama was performed; but this play on which the manipulators had labored for many months was abandoned because of too great difficulty in manipulating . . . and because of other complications which shall be nameless.

MARIONETTES

One of the plays we produced was *Shadowy Waters* by Yeats, a dreamy, far-away, old Irish drama which lent itself beautifully to our type of poetic puppets. Mr. John Black designed the colorful costumes and the scene upon the deck of a vessel. The pleasure of making and dressing the impressionistic dolls was delegated to me, but all willing members of the group were allowed to share in this privilege. There were five longsuffering readers and four patient operators, besides the director of the group, who also manipulated, with extra assistance, at the very end, to carry the marionettes back and forth behind the scene. Mr. O'Neil also generously helped in staging the production. Many and varied were the rehearsal evenings we spent together. But, when at last the curtain slowly fell upon the Queen in her turquoise gown with "hair the color of burning" and her dark, melancholy lover beside her, deserted by the sailors and drifting away over shadowy blue waters to the strains of the magic harp, we all felt that we had created something of beauty, despite our inexperience and obvious shortcomings.

The other puppet play was somewhat in the nature of a departure at the Playhouse. A little narrative of the life of Chopin, written by Mr. Albert Gehring, was read to the accompaniment of piano selections from Chopin's music while dainty little figures of the period, gently moving, enacted the scenes in the story as it proceeded. This method has had many and ancient precedents in the ambulent puppet shows of

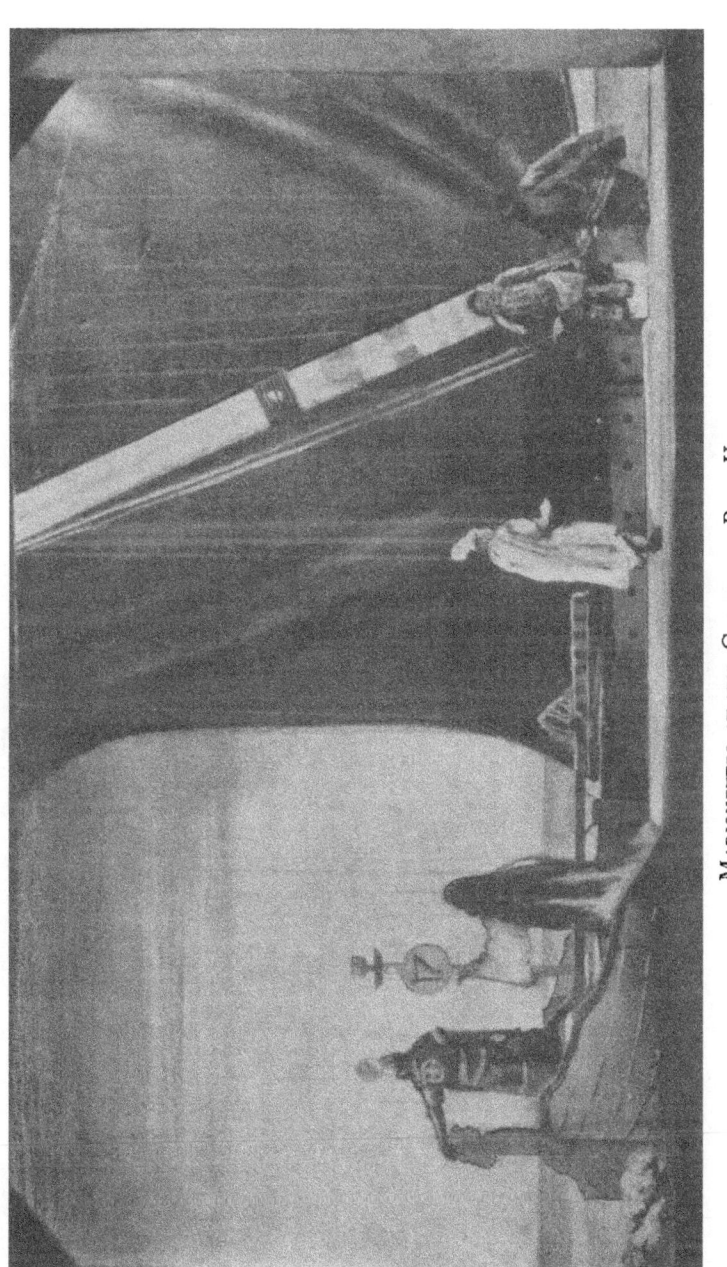

Marionettes at the Cleveland Play House
Production of *Shadowy Waters* by W. B. Yeats
Puppets and scenery designed by John Black

the Middle Ages. The success of the experiment has suggested to some puppeteers in the group the idea of further attempts in this manner. Mr. Carl Broemel was the artist who designed the elegantly clad and exquisite little dolls, as well as the setting for the play. The latter was a remarkable example of a miniature interior which, despite its diminutive furnishings, had nothing petty about it but gave one the unified, powerful effect of a dignified painting, poetically and simply conceived.

Thus the Cleveland puppets have struggled along through hard days of war and worries, very much alive although perhaps less active than they may hope some day to be. Plans have been made to start rehearsing a play longer and more important than the recent endeavors, (possibly Hauptmann's *Hannele*). The problem of a permanent marionette theatre depending upon volunteer workers is unbelievably difficult, but we feel that with time the solution can be found not only for our group but for other communities as well who may venture upon this fascinating minor branch of dramatic endeavor.[1]

To New York accrues the credit of having to-day professional marionettes on exhibition in a theatre on Broadway. Created by the inventive genius of

[1] Mr. Alfred Kreymborg informs me that *Lima Beans*, one of his amusing little poem-mimes, was played by puppets in Los Angeles, under the direction of Miss Vivian Aiken. Mr. Kreymborg has written that he considers "the only possible approach to a Synthetic stage is derived from the marionette performance." Of the puppeteers in Los Angeles, one would like to hear more.

Mr. Tony Sarg, and sustained through the sympathetic interest of Mr. Winthrop Ames, these most accomplished and amazing dolls made their debut at the Neighborhood Playhouse over a year ago, whence, after arousing great enthusiasm, they moved into the Punch and Judy Theatre. There, before an audience of appreciative big and little folk, they performed three tales of fable and fantasia, or as the headlines of a newspaper described it, after the manner of the old advertisements: "Master marionettes of new Refinements. Strangely Human Semblance and Various Illusion . . . Tale and Whimsey."

The story of these marionettes began over five years ago in London, where Mr. Sarg had his studio in *The Old Curiosity Shop*, made famous by Dickens. There he worked at his illustrating and played with his puppets. The performances he gave for the amusement of himself and his friends encouraged him in becoming more and more absorbed in the miniature stage. After the war had broken out, Mr. Sarg came to New York and brought his marionettes along. Here he continued his professional activities, illustrating diligently and most successfully, with interludes of puppet play. When, finally, Mr. Ames became interested in presenting these puppets to the public, it was found necessary to enlarge and elaborate upon the original pattern, and after many months of experimenting, patient labor and happy inspiration, Mr. Sarg perfected the ingenious, three-foot marionettes used in these first public productions.

Mr. Tony Sarg's Marionettes behind the Scenes

Each of his thirty-six or more little figures was designed with an eye to its special uses; some require as many as twenty-four strings for the manipulating. One of the little figures is a masterpiece of flexibility. Of her it has been written: "This doll is an Oriental dancer. Her contortions and posturings are in perfect imitation of the living Nautch-girl and it is safe to say that nothing ever seen on the puppet stage of America at least can surpass the ease and grace with which her little body sways backward in an inverted crescent, the ethereal lightness of her circling about the stage and the abandon of her attitudes in the dance." Another critic comments with an almost audible chuckle: ". . . a nine days' marvel and most improper. She pains and shocks all right thinking people by her shameless display of those allurements against which all the prophets have warned the sons of men."

I myself was even more impressed by Mr. Sarg's puppet-juggler. He is an adorable little expert, tossing and catching his many golden balls with such tense, nervous concern, jerking his head left and right to watch first this hand, then that, then a ball high in air and, having accomplished his trick, he stands with such justifiable pride and swelling of chest to receive the well-earned plaudits of the audience! It was a quite irresistible bit of mimicry. There is, indeed, a nice humor and an enjoyable but not overemphasized flavor of the grotesque in these marionettes. Heads, hands and feet are a little exaggerated in proportion to the rest of the body; added to this, the ease with which they accomplish the humanly impossible and the difficulty with which they perform some very trivial and ordinary human acts all bring about a curious absurdity which is highly amusing.

Of the three plays presented the opening season, the first was *The Three Wishes,* an old fairy tale dramatized by Count F. Pocci for the marionette theatre of Papa Schmidt in Munich and readapted by Mr. Ames. "The tiny stage," writes Miss Anne Stoddard, "is set in a shadow box; the curtain rises on a sunny knoll with a glimpse of red roofs in the valley below; bright butterflies flutter above the grass; a saucy Molly cotton-tail bobs across the hillside." Another witness of the performance continues: "The supernatural is a ready aid to the marionette drama. Hence one is not surprised to find in the first play of Mr. Sarg's entertainment a fairy being released from an imprisoning tree by an old woodcutter and offering her liberator the familiar three wishes. The tale bears one of the morals familiar in German folklore. The woodcutter, having received his wish-ring, is awed by the responsibility which rests upon him and rushes to consult with the wife of his bosom. She is equally perturbed, but guards the ring for him while he departs to hold conference with the schoolmaster, but how perverse is human nature! The wife, entertaining a neighbor during his absence, casually expresses the wish for a plate of sausages. Presto, sausages hot and tempting appear before her. The woodcutter, returning and discovering what use his wife has made of the first wish, angrily wishes the sausages were growing at the end of her nose, and lo, so they are. The third wish still remains. But what will avail all the honor and wealth in the world if one's wife is to make one ridiculous by carrying sausages on the end of her nose? Clearly there is nothing to be done but to utilize the third wish in wishing the sausages off again. And, this accomplished, the fairy appears to preach a homely sermon, pointing out how vain are human wishes and ambitions. Let each gain what he would have by his own will and industry and be contented with the lot he carves for himself.

"The edifying import of this tale is no less impressive than the spirited enactment of it, — the grace of the fairy, the ardor of the woodcutter, the nagging of the wife, the fervent emotion displayed by the housedog at the smell of the sausages. Such a mingling of fable, parable and sermon, of petty human nature with the inscrutable supernatural which hedges us all in is the authentic material of puppet-drama."

The other two plays, expertly written by Mrs. Hamilton Williamson, displayed to the greatest advantage the particular talents of the puppet virtuosi. It is thus that she depicts the task of the marionette dramatist. "When Mr. Sarg first told me he wanted a snake-charmer, a juggler, an Oriental dancer, an elephant and a donkey in one play, I thought I couldn't possibly get them together; but, you see, I did." Yes, indeed, and more besides in the way of adventure, mystery and humor, very cleverly devised in the energetic, simple language best suited to the naïve audience of puppet actors. Nor did the duties of Mrs. Williamson end with her literary labors. Many and inspired were her humbler but equally arduous and indispensable achievements for these puppets.

A similar versatility was displayed by the young women who operated the puppets. Aside from the laboriously acquired precision essential in mastering the intricate controls devised for the dolls, each puppeteer has interested herself in other phases of the ancient craft. Some of them made the elaborate and colorful costumes for the dolls. Some helped manufacture the properties, tiny but complete and delightful. My very first glimpse of the marvelous puppets, indeed, was when, led by Mrs. Williamson, I came to a very dirty brownstone house not far from Washington Square, and, entering a gloomy hallway, penetrated through into the dark rear room where the puppeteers were at work, all in overalls, all very busy, all very amiable. Someone was sawing wood, someone was hammering, someone was up on the bridge practicing the donkey and there was a tiny, live monkey perched on the lumber which littered the floor. Puppets and monkey . . . of course! — following the example of Brioche and his Fagotin and perfectly true to the best traditions!

It is Mr. Sarg who has trained and inspired all of

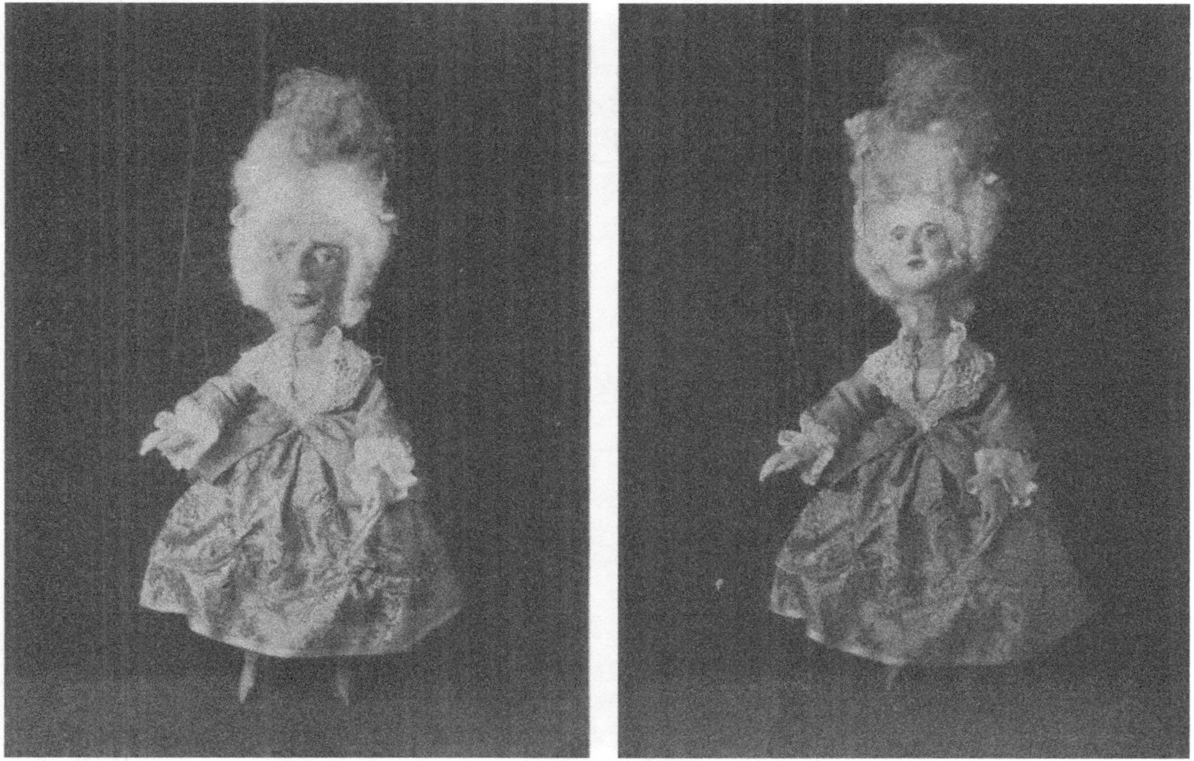

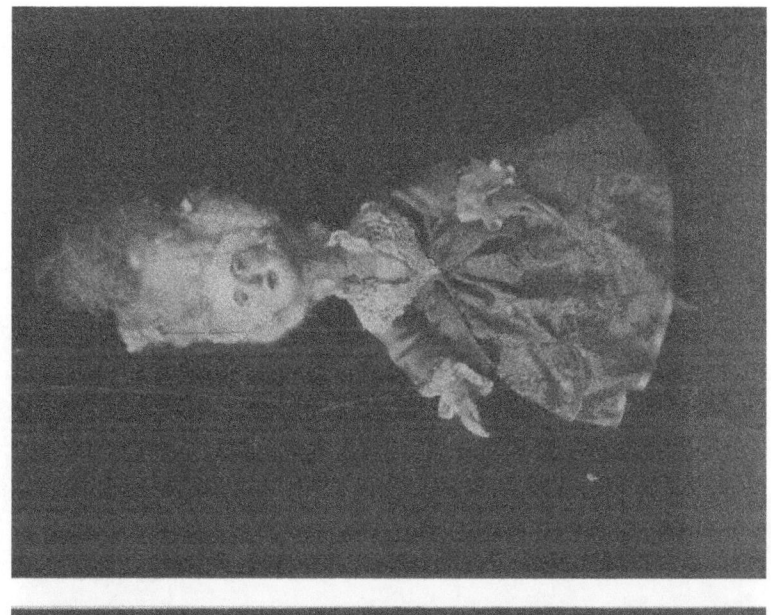

A Trick Puppet

In Mr. Tony Sarg's production, *The Rose and the Ring*; showing how Gruffanuff becomes instantly beautiful upon finding the magic ring

his workers, who has designed the costumes as well as the faces and hands of the dolls, modeled after his drawings, who has invented the clever mechanism and most of the scenery and ingenious "business" of the stage, who has directed the actors' interpretation of the lines, selected the incidental music, superintended the lighting effects, all with an easy air of merely enjoying his little hobby.

The play selected by Mr. Sarg for his puppets during their second season was a very fortunate choice. It was Thackeray's little fairy story, *The Rose and the Ring*, made into a drama by one of the puppeteers, Miss Hettie Louise Mick, who had dramatized other tales for marionettes when she was working with the Chicago puppets. Nothing could have been better suited to the nature of Mr. Sarg's dolls, humorous, dainty, delicious, all in quaint trappings, and with divertingly elaborate settings suggestive of the Victorian era quite proper to the story. To add to the excellence of his production, Mr. Sarg secured Mrs. Browne to advise in staging and to direct the rehearsing. She applied her usual methods, training the puppeteers first through having them act out and speak the lines themselves before operating the dolls. The manipulators always talk for the marionettes they operate.

To facilitate in taking the show about the country a collapsible stage was constructed and the puppets were reduced in size. This diminution of stature brought about a new refinement, a more mincing manner and a more piquant facial eccentricity. Early in Spring, *The Rose and The Ring* went on a Western tour, visiting Detroit, Ann Arbor and Cleveland. Mr. Sarg had a group of six manipulators, including Miss Lillian Owen, mistress of the wardrobe and a sort of right-hand man, and Mr. Searle, master stage mechanic and constructor of clever scenery and properties, another right-hand man in fact, and Miss Mick, who wrote the play. A musician also came along and produced the tinkly, tinny, toy music so properly attuned to the puppet play. The production abounded in pretty surprises, horrible suspenses, fairy magic, transformations, shadow play, dancing dolls, piano playing puppets, knights in armor, animals, everything desirable! Throughout there was the flow of Thackeray's. inimitable, good-natured satire, skillfully preserved by Miss Mick. After enthusiastic receptions wherever he visited with them, Mr. Sarg returned to New York with his marionettes and installed them in the Punch and Judy theatre, where they continued to enjoy their usual popularity.

Mr. Sarg has been asked why he does not attempt poetic drama with his marionettes. He is faced, of course, with the problem which confronts all the puppet showmen here in America of finding material suitable for a given type of doll and also acceptable to local audiences, hitherto unacquainted with the characteristics and traditions of the burattini. Concerning a possible performance of one of Maeterlinck's dramas by the marionettes, Mr. Sarg has said: "I am turning that over in my mind. The practicable difficulty is the exaggerated walk of the dolls, which always brings laughter from the audience. But I dare say I can manage that all right when I have a chance to work over it a bit." Let us hope that this minor difficulty will not prove insurmountable, for, as Mr. H. K. Moderwell in the *Boston Transcript* has so aptly written: "If he will draw further from the ancient and noble sources of puppet literature, if he will bid his dolls enact some of those dramas which have made the art of the marionette an inspired art, he will merit the plaudits of all puppet-starved America."

Toy Theatres and Puppet Shows for Children

WHETHER, out of their infinite variety, the puppets please or fail to satisfy us, there is one audience invariably eager for them. Puppet shows for children, toy theatres managed by children, what could be more fitting? Specially adapted, professional performances such as the Guignol and Casperle plays have ever catered to youthful tastes with astonishing and perennial success. The home-made booths for simple dolls worked on the fingers are so quickly contrived. Little stages for marionettes are easy to construct out of ordinary kitchen tables. Mr. Gordon Craig gives explicit directions as well as an excellent drawing in his letter, *The Game of Marionettes*, which is published in *The Mask*, volume five. Shadow plays can be arranged by merely stretching a sheet across a door with a cardboard frame and cardboard figures pressed behind it and a light to illuminate the silhouettes. How much fun to have Red Riding Hood thus portrayed, for a birthday party or the shadow of Santa Claus with his reindeer sailing over the shadow gables and down the shadow of the chimney on Christmas eve!

MARIONETTES

The *Juvenile Drama* of Skelt and his successors, Park, Webb, Redington and Pollock, has been immortalized by Stevenson in his little essay, *A Penny Plain and Twopence Colored*. Printed on thin sheets of cardboard to be cut out and colored by the youthful stage manager (unless he bought, oh shame! the *Twopence Colored*), were characters and scenes for the most exciting plays. Special properties for illuminating and coloring could be acquired also, at extra expense. The words of the drama, plus directions, were printed in a pamphlet. They were based upon thrilling old English melodramas; they presented startling and highly theatrical situations.

"In the Leith Walk window all the year round, there stood displayed a theatre in working order, with a *Forest Set*, a *Combat*, and a few *Robbers Carousing* in the slides; and below and about, dearer tenfold to me! the plays themselves, those budgets of romance, lay tumbled one upon the other. Long and often have I lingered there with empty pockets. One figure, we shall say, was visible in the first plate of characters, bearded, pistol in hand, or drawing to his ear the clothyard arrow. I would spell the name: was it Macaire or Long Tom Coffin, or Grindoff, 2d dress? Oh, how I would long to see the rest! How — if the name by chance were hidden — I would wonder in what play he figured and what immortal legend justified his attitude and strange apparel! And then to go within to announce yourself as an intending purchaser, and, closely watched, be suffered to undo those bundles and to breathlessly devour those pages of gesticulating villains, epileptic combats, bosky forests, palaces and warships, frowning fortresses and prison vaults — it was a giddy joy."

"And when at length the deed was done, the play selected and the impatient shopman had brushed the rest into the gray portfolio, and the boy was forth again, a little late for dinner, the lamps springing into light in the blue winter's even, and *The Miller*, or *The Rover*, or some kindred drama clutched against his side, on what gay feet he ran, and how he laughed aloud in exultation!" And Stevenson confesses: "I have, at different times, possessed *Aladdin, The Red Rover, The Blind Boy, The Old Oak Chest, The Wood Daemon, Jack Shepard, The Miller and His Men, Der Freischuetz, The Smuggler, The Forest of Bondy, Robin Hood, The Waterman, Richard I., My Poll and my Partner Joe, The Inchcape Bell* (imperfect), and *Three-fingered Jack the Terror of Jamaica;* and I have assisted others in the illumination of the *Maid of the Inn* and *The Battle of Waterloo.* In this rollcall of stirring names you read the evidences of a happy childhood." [1]

In Germany, also, toy theaters abound, better equipped possibly, and more carefully constructed,

[1] Mr. B. Pollock, 73 Hoxton St., London, writes: "I still publish Juvenile Plays and also supply foot lights and tin slides which are used with the theatre. I have now been carrying on the business for forty-two years and my father-in-law about thirty-eight years before me."

but lacking somewhat the quaint and fiery delightfulness of the English juvenile drama.

There could be no more spontaneous testimonial of the love of children for the puppets than the throngs who crowded into Papa Schmidt's Kasperle theatre to witness his familiar, jolly little shows of fairy-tale and folklore. In striving to meet the tastes and needs of children, Schmidt earned the reward of becoming the best beloved man in the city. It is interesting to note that when, once, he became discouraged and wished to retire, the city magistrates, urged by the *superintendent of the schools*, unanimously voted to build him a permanent little theatre.

And Goethe, that German genius of most universal appeal, records that he devoted many hours of his childhood to puppet play. Kept at home during the dreary days of the Seven Years' War when Frankfurt was occupied by the French, he diverted not only himself but his family with the little marionette theatre which he had received as a Christmas gift. It is thus that he describes his introduction to the puppets who were to delight his boyhood, to amuse his youth and to inspire him eventually with the suggestion for his great Faust drama.

"I can still see the moment — how wonderful it seemed — when, after the usual Christmas presents, we were told to sit down before a door which led from one room into another. It opened, but not merely for the usual passing in and out; the entrance was filled with an unexpected festiveness. A portal reared itself into the heights which was covered by a mystic curtain. At first we marvelled from a distance and as our curiosity became greater to see what glittering and rustling things might be concealed behind the half-transparent drapery, a little chair was assigned to each of us and we were told to wait in patience.

"So then we all sat down and were quiet. A whistle gave signal, the curtain rose and disclosed a scene in the Temple, painted bright red. The High Priest Samuel appeared with Jonathan, and their curious dialogue seemed most admirable to me. Shortly thereafter Saul came upon the scene in great distress, over the insolence of the heavy-weight warrior who had challenged him and his followers to combat. How relieved I was when the diminutive son of Jesse sprang forth with shepherd's crook, wallet and sling and spoke thus: 'Almighty King and great Lord! Let none despair because of this. If your Majesty will permit me, I will go forth and enter into combat with the mighty giant.' The first act was ended and the audience extremely desirous to learn what would happen next," etc., etc.

The puppets may indeed boast of having delighted child geniuses of every country and of having inspired their later years. We are told that at the age of eleven Stanislaw Wyspianski, the great poet, painter and dramatist of Poland, built himself a large stage or *Crib* imitating architecturally the Castle of Wawel. On this stage he produced various dramas based upon the history of that royal burg, with the help of figures

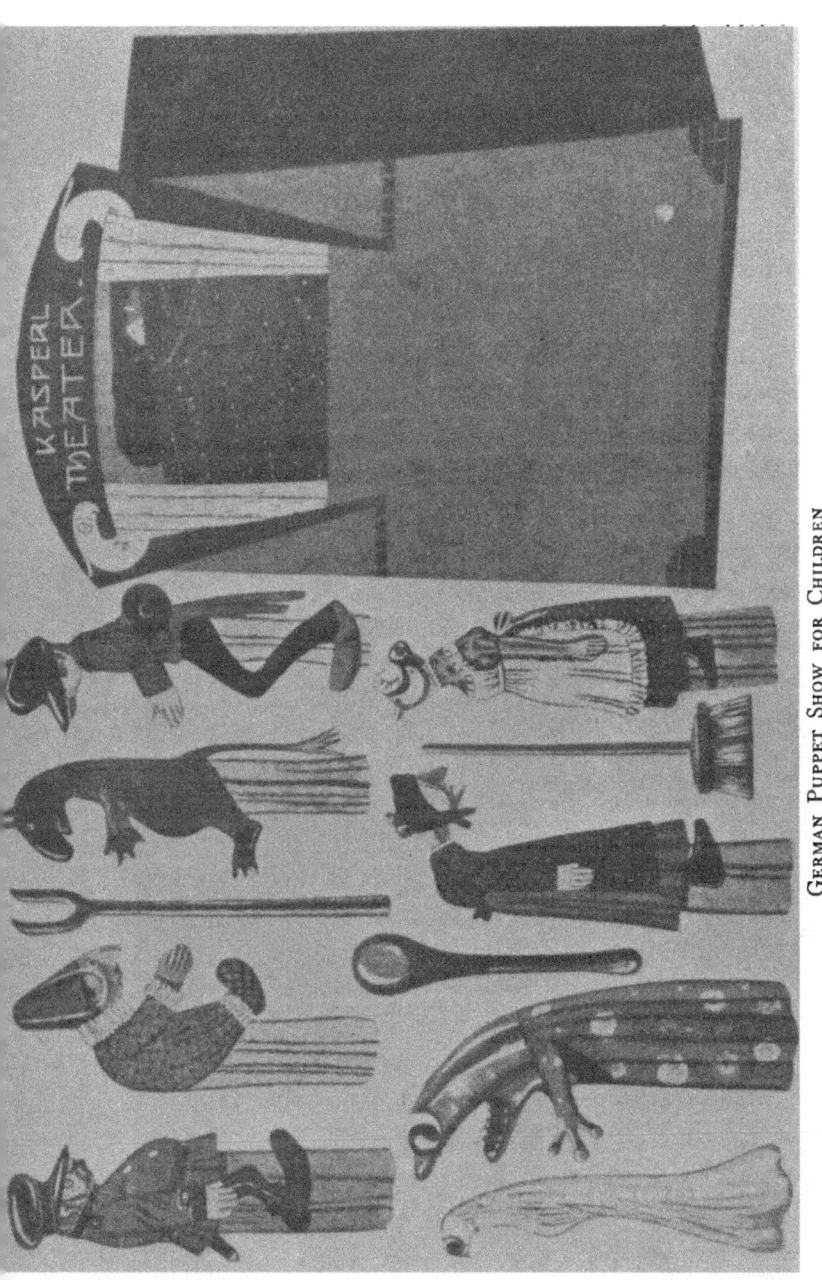

GERMAN PUPPET SHOW FOR CHILDREN
Designed for use in the home
[Reproduced from *Kind und Kunst*]

which he himself invented. "Perhaps," his biographer suggests, "already there was germinating in his boyish soul the idea of the Theatre-Wawel which in his manly productiveness brought forth manifold fruits." (L. de Schildenfeld Schiller.) In Italy, too, we find the great dramatist Goldoni devoted to puppet play as á child and writing dramas for the burattini which he is said to have adapted later, with great success, for the larger stage.

Most famous, perhaps, of all popular puppets for children to-day are the Guignols in Paris. A typical performance might be found in the garden of the Luxembourg, where a little stage has been erected. One has the privilege of standing outside the roped-off space with passing pastry cooks, milliners' girls and street urchins, or one may pay to enter and sit down on a chair among the children and nurses. Coachmen rein up and watch from their high perches at the curb. Polichinelle first comes upon the stage with his piping voice, or the Director, a doll in evening dress with waxed mustachios, welcomes the audience. Then Guignol and the terrifying family scenes!

Mr. W. Caine has given a very illuminating analysis of the guignols. "But who are all these people? Guignol, Guillaume, the Judge, the Patron, the Nurse? You might know that Guignol is Guillaume's father, while Guillaume is the son of Guignol. The Gendarme, on the other hand, is the Gendarme, while the Judge, similarly, is the Judge. The Patron is none other than the Patron, and who should the Nurse be, in the name of common sense, but the Nurse? The Gendarme is always killed, always. The Judge expends his wrath impotently, always. The Patron is invariably worsted, the Nurse has no sort of luck. Guignol represents the proletariat. He wears a dark green jacket and a black hat . . . His face is large and foolish, for he is what is known as a benet, a simpleton. . . . He tries to give his own baby its dinner by thrusting it head-first into a stewing pan. Guillaume wears a red hat and pink blouse. . . . Guillaume is, in one word, a rascal. It is certain when once Guillaume gets hold of a stick, or musket, or a stewing-pan (anything will do) that somebody will bite the dust."

The enthusiasm of the juvenile audience grows most intense over the exploits of this favorite, and it is not unusual when Guillaume is sore put to it and the Gendarme is about to pounce upon him, to hear a shrill little voice from the audience cry out, 'Take care, Guillaume, the Gendarme is behind the door!' When for the first time the adventurous Guillaume ascended in an aeroplane, so great was his success that the price of seats in the Champs Elysees went from 10 centimes to 25!!"

Guignol is often to be found during the season at bathing resorts and at the seashore. Each of the larger shows in Paris has a portable booth belonging to it wherein its little cast can be sent out to perform at private entertainments. It is not uncommon for the play to be sent to the orphans and waifs in this manner as a special treat for fête days.

MARIONETTES

We find the puppets equally beloved by the children of Italy. In *The Marionette* there is a sympathetic picture of a juvenile audience at the theatre of the Lupi family in Torina. "On the evenings of ordinary days the auditorium does not differ in aspect from that of the other theatres. To see it in its especial beauty one must go to the Sunday afternoon performance, when hundreds of boys and girls fill the seats and benches, and form, in the *platea* and the boxes, so many bouquets, garlands of blond heads; and the variety of light bright colors of their clothes give it the appearance of a sala decked with flowers and flags for a fête.

"On the rising of the curtain one may say that two performances begin. It is delightful, during a spectacular scene, to see all those eyes wide open as at an apparition from another world — those expressions of the most supreme amazement, in which life seems suspended — those little mouths open in the form of an O, or of rings and semicircles — those little foreheads corrugated as if in a tremendous effort of philosophic cogitation, which then relax brusquely as on awaking from a dream. Then, all at once, at a comic scene, at a funny reply or action of one of the characters, whole rows of little bodies double up with laughter, lines of heads are thrown back, shaking masses of curls, disclosing little white necks, opening mouths, like little red caskets full of minute pearls; and in the impetus of their delight some embrace their brother or sister, some throw themselves in their mother's arms, and many of the smallest fling themselves back in their seats with their legs in the air, innocently disclosing their most secret *lingerie*. And then, to see how in the passion of admiration they furiously push aside the importunate handkerchief which seeks their little noses, or deal a blow without preface to whoever hides from them the view of the stage! There are three hundred pairs of hands that applaud with all their might, and that, among them all, do not make as much noise as four men's hands; one seems to see and to hear the flutter of hundreds of rosy wings, held by so many threads to the seats.

"And the admiring and enthusiastic exclamations are a joy to hear. At the unexpected opening of certain scenes, at the appearance of certain lambs or little donkeys or pigs that seem alive, there are outbursts of 'Oh!' and long murmurs of wonder, behind which comes almost always some solitary exclamation of a little voice which resounds in the silence like a sigh in a church, and. . . 'Ah, com'e bello!' . . . that breaks from the depths of the soul, that expresses fulness of content, a celestial beatitude."

When Mr. Tony Sarg brought *The Rose and The Ring* west it was a rare privilege for the children of Cleveland to see this winsome puppet play and an equal pleasure for those elders who witnessed the performance with them. *What* was behind the little curtain? A few boys and girls went tiptoe up to peek. Then, listen! there is music and then, oh! the funny

ENGLISH TOY THEATRE
Upper: Figures to be cut out for the Juvenile Dramas
Lower: Back scene for *Timour the Tartar*
[Courtesy of B. Pollock, 73 Hoxton Street, London]

little man singing a song, and oh! the long-nosed little King snoring on his throne, and the funny soldier, Hedsoff, saluting so briskly, and the ugly old Lady Gruffanuff! And see the Fairy Blackstick come floating in and do things and say things to people and Princess Angelica playing piano and dancing. How can she, so little and only a dolly? What a fat Prince Bulbo and oh, the armoured men on horseback fighting! ("Why ha' dey dose knives, Mudda?" questioned one little girl, aloud, all unacquainted with the days of Chivalry). And then the roaring Lion! My four-year-old daughter still calls the lion a bear: but it pleased her notwithstanding, particularly the *roar* of it. "Oh, I just juve Mr. Sarg's ma-inette dolls, Mudda," she exclaimed, a day after the blissful event. "Why don't we have ma-inette dolls many times?" Why indeed, or, why not?!

Elnora Whitman Curtis, in her book *The Dramatic Instinct in Education*, emphasizes the educational value of puppets. She would have shows in the schools, or better yet, in playgrounds with the advantage of fresh air. Subjects, she claims, could be vivified, literature and history lessons more deeply impressed upon the great number of pupils who never get beyond the grades. And for older children there would be the training in the writing of dialogues, in the declaiming of them, practice in fashioning the puppets, the costumes, the scenery, the properties and in operating and directing. Miss Curtis concludes: "Anyone who has watched a throng of small boys and girls as they sit in the tiny, roped-off square before a little chatelet in Paris on the Champs Élysées, or those that gather in Papa Schmidt's exquisite little theatre in Munich, or before the tiny booths at fairs and exhibitions anywhere in Italy, must have noticed the rapturous delight of these small people. The tiny stage, its equipment, accessories, the diminutive garments and belongings of the puppets satisfy the childish love of the miniature copies of things in the grown-up world. Their animistic tendencies make it easy to endow the wooden figures with human qualities and bring them into close rapport with their own world of fancy. The voice coming from some unknown region adds the mystery which children dearly love, and before the magic of fairy-tales their eyes grow wide with wonder. The stiff movement of the puppets, their sudden collapses from dignity, are irresistibly funny to the little people and the element of buffoonery is doubly comical in its mechanical presentation."

Less specifically, but with equal conviction of their deep educational importance, Gordon Craig proclaims: "There is one way in which to assist the world to become young again. It is to allow the young mind to learn nearly all things from the marionette."

A Plea for Polichinelle

I AM making a plea for Polichinelle and I hope I shall be pardoned for summoning to my assistance some of his more eloquent and illustrious admirers. We have seen that the past has eminently honored him, but there is also ample testimony that he can adapt himself to our present time and taste, nay more, to the various tastes and tempers of this modern day. For there are divers theories and principles among critics of the puppets, but the puppets are so versatile they can play many parts in many manners. "Chacun a son gout!" quoth Polichinelle with a flourish.

There are those who believe that the grotesque is an inherent, indispensable trait of the marionette; that, as Flögel claims, Kasperle, quintessence of grotesque comedy, belongs inseparably to the marionette stage and that everything else is meaningless, insipid, and merely experimental. Similarly, Professor Wundt asserts that the ministration to the sense of the comic is the chief function of the puppets and perhaps the greatest factor in their popularity. He mentions their mirth-provoking superiority to the situation, the element of the unexpected, heightened enormously by wooden creatures who imperturbably proceed upon occasions to contradict the very law of gravity. These traits, he feels, are essential and distinguishing characteristics of marionettes.

In comparing the merry Kasperle theatre of Munich with the serious puppet theatre established by the young artists of that city, Wilhelm Michel emphasizes this point of view. "Pure tragic effects cannot emanate from the marionette stage because, in the first place, there are no human beings acting upon it but rather ironies of humanity, mockeries of men; suffering cannot be given upon it, only travesties of suffering. If this constitutional irony of the puppet is not handled in an artistic spirit, unbearable dissonances occur. . . . The working of the marionette stage is pure, unmixed gayety. The dolls are not, as our young poets imagine, representatives and agents of submission, but rather delightful little liberators, amiable, amusing victors over the petty doubts which we all carry about with us in unobserved corners of our souls."

This opinion is undeniably supported by traditional usage. Humor may vary from the buffoonery of Hanswurst to the satirical subtleties of De Neuville's pupazzi, but the spirit of comedy has had a representative on the puppet stage in every land. What a long list might be compiled, starting with the hunchback Vidusaka of ancient India, then on through Semar of Javanese comedy, Karagheuz of Turkey, Pahlawan of Persia (squeaking in the same feigned voice as the English Punch), to say nothing of Maccus, the Roman Puppet, and Arlecchino, and Pulcinella with their merry train from all over Italy, even including the later Signor Macaroni. There are the German and Austrian Hanswurst and Kasperle, Jackpudding and Punch in England, Polichinelle, Harlequin, Jean Potage, and even more recently Guignol and Guillaume in France, Paprika, Jancsi of Hungary, Picklehoerring of Holland and ever so many more, rollicking and indispensable humorists of the puppet theatre. M. Charles Magnin, most distinguished historian of the marionette, proclaims his unalterable faith in Polichinelle: "Do you know, then, what Polichinelle is? He is the good sense of the people, the brisk sally, the irrepressible laughter. Yes, Polichinelle will laugh and sing as long as the world contains vices, follies and things to ridicule. You see very well that Polichinelle is not near his death. Polichinelle is immortal!"

Professor Pischel agrees that the puppet play is the favorite child of the people and merely the step-child of the cultured because it owes its origin to the common people and is a clearer mirror of their thoughts and feelings than any more finished poetry. Mr. Howard, too, in the *Boston Transcript*, somewhat resents the marionette performances in the new manner, feeling that the old traditional shows were "more childlike, more simple, more human."

Innumerable artists of the last few decades, ever, esteem the marionette as an excellent medium of serious dramatic expression, possessing a poetic style and a conventionalized, impersonal symbolism.

Ernst Ehlert, himself an actor as well as lover of puppets, writes thus of Puhony's marionettes:

"The object of every work of art, the thing that makes it truly artistic, is the attainment of the greatest possible emotional effect with the simplest possible means. What makes a work of art a real delight is that it does not fully express but merely suggests and excites the imagination of the observer to help in the presentation of the reality. That is why a puppet play is not only more amusing but more artistic than a real one. He continues: "Puppets, moreover, have style. They are cut out sharply to represent their particular characteristics, and those characteristics are pronounced. The manager of a puppet show has a free hand in the fashioning of such a company as best carries out his creative impulse. But with real actors it is impossible to make them other than they are, to subordinate them entirely to the manager's will. I have been an actor, both in Germany and in Russia . . . so I know."

Again, Mr. Arthur Symons, after witnessing the fantoccini of the Cortanzi theatre in Rome, expresses the following belief in the art-marionette: "Gesture on the stage is the equivalent of rhythm in verse. In our marionette, then, we get personified gesture, and the gesture, like all forms of emotion, generalized. The appeal in what seems to you these childlike manoeuvers is to a finer because to a more intimately poetic sense of things than the merely rationalistic appeal of our modern plays." Furthermore, he adds concerning the puppet: "As he is painted so he will smile, as the wires lift or lower his hands so will his gestures be and he will dance when his legs are set in motion. There is not, indeed, the appeal to the senses of the first row in the stalls at a ballet of living dancers. But why leave the ball-room? It is not nature one looks for on the stage in this kind of a spectacle, and our excitement in watching it should remain purely intellectual. This is nothing less than a fantastic and direct return to the masks of the ancient Greeks, that learned artifice by which tragedy and comedy were assisted in speaking to the world in the universal voice by this deliberate generalizing of emotions."

The marionettes of M. Signoret, as we have seen, from Anatole France's enthusiastic account, presented the classic drama of all epochs to the satisfaction of the most acutely sensitive critics of Paris. M. Paul Margueritte brilliantly eulogizes them in the following discussion: "They are indefatigable, always ready. And while the name and too familiar face of a living actor imposes upon the public an obsession which renders illusion impossible or very difficult, the puppets being of wood or cardboard possess a droll, mysterious life. Their truthful bearing surprises, even disquiets us. In their essential gestures there is the complete expression of human feelings. We had it proved at the representations of Aristophanes; real actors would not have produced this effect. In them the foreshortening aided the illusion. Their masks in the style of ancient comedy, their few and simple movements, their statuesque poses, gave a singular grace to the spectacle."

This leads us to the well-known name of Gordon Craig and to his inspired, emphatic utterances concerning the actor and the marionette. No one of late has done as much as he toward reviving the interest in puppets and stimulating curiosity concerning them. His collection of puppets and shadow figures forms a veritable museum of marionettes from all parts of the world. His many articles in *The Mask* and in a later publication called *The Marionettes*, both published in Florence at the Arena Goldoni, direct attention to the puppet; — more, it must be admitted, as a model or suggestion to the actor, than as a minor art-form in itself. Recognizing its many merits, Mr. Craig would send the modern actor to the school of the burattini to learn virtues of silence, obedience, "to learn how to indicate instead of imitate." He deems the stage of to-day devoid, in great part, of genuine dramatic value, filled up with much meaningless realistic detail, inartistic and irritating gestures, and prominent players exhibiting their own peculiar personalities more or less attractively in various rôles. He would agree with Anatole France: "The actors spoil the play for me. I mean good actors, — their talent is too great; it covers everything. There is nothing left but them. Their personality effaces the work which they represent." Indeed, Gordon Craig boldly proclaims: "The actor must go and in his

MARIONETTES

place comes the inanimate figure, the Über-marionette we may call him until he has won for himself a better name." And in *The Promise of a New Art* he has written: "What the wires of the Über-marionette shall be, who shall guide him? — The wires which stretch from Divinity to the soul of the poet are wires which might command him."

These sentiments are familiar to those acquainted with the art and writings of Mr. Craig, but it is indeed interesting to find somewhat similar ideas expressed in the delightful but "different" manner of a most eminent contemporary, Mr. G. Bernard Shaw. In a letter concerning the puppets of his acquaintance, Mr. Shaw has written: "In my youth (say 1865-75) there was a permanent exhibition in Dublin, the proprietor of which was known as Mons Dark, which is Irish for Monsieur d'Arc. From that show I learned that marionettes can produce a much stronger illusion than bad actors can; and I have often suggested that the Academy of Dramatic Art here try to obtain a marionette performance to teach the students that very important part of the art of acting which consists of not acting: that is, allowing the imagination of the spectator to do its lion's share of the work."

Aside, however, from this not insignificant value as an example to the actor of the future, the marionette has a positive and individual contribution to make in the field of drama, a contribution which the marionette alone can provide. There seem to be certain types of plays more advantageously presented by puppets or shadows than by human beings. These little creatures of wood or cardboard have naturally that "sense of being beyond reality" which, according to John Balance, "permeates all good art." There is an article in the *Hyperion, 1909*, by Franz Blei, critic and aesthete. He states: "I believe there will always be certain dramatic poetry whose beauty can be more significantly and effectively revealed by shadows than by living actors. The shadow play will supplement the theatre of living actors on one side as the marionette stage already does on the other, in Paul Brann's very brilliant productions, for example. With shadows, the forcefulness of the verse and the emotional element is very much heightened in effect; with marionettes the significance of the action is intensified to a far greater degree than is attainable by human beings, a point to which H. V. Kleist has already drawn attention in praise of marionettes. With shadow plays, as with puppet performances, the readers should not be professional actors, for their very way of speaking invariably mimics the mannerisms of the man. The limited movements of the shadows, however, suffer from this and also the gestures of the marionettes which have a wider range but which do not in the least resemble the customary stage gestures. Talented dilettantes with good taste are more apt to strike the right note. I fancy that the shadows and marionettes might please some people who had not visited the theatre for quite a while, because they were unwilling to waste their time on highly lifelike but utterly lifeless theatrical productions."

Professor Brander Matthews, in his *Book about the Theatre*, also insists upon the adaptability of the marionettes for certain types of drama unsatisfactory when performed by living actors. He suggests that a passion play or any form of drama in which Divinity has perforce to appear is relieved in the puppet show of any tincture of irreverence, all personages of the play, whether heavenly or earthly, appearing equally remote from common humanity upon the miniature stage. The religious plays of Maurice Bouchor, artistic and reverent productions in every detail, beautifully illustrate this point. The atmosphere M. Jules Lemaître describes as "far away in time and space," — this of the mystery play, *Noël*. Again Professor Matthews maintains that when *Salome* was performed by Holden's marionettes and created the sensation of the season, all vulgarity and grossness which might have been offensive either in the play or in the dance of the seven veils was purged away by the fact that the performers were puppets. "So dextrous was the manipulation of the unseen operator who controlled the wires and strings which gave life to the seductive Salome as she circled around the stage in a most bewitching fashion; so precise and accurate was the imitation of a human dancer, that the receptive spectator could not but feel that here at last a play of doubtful propriety has found its only fit stage and its only proper performance. The memory of that exhibition is a perennial delight to all those who possess it. A thing of beauty it was and it abides in remembrance as a joy forever. It revealed the art of the puppet show at its summit. And the art itself was eternally justified by that one performance of the highest technical skill and the utmost delicacy of taste."

There are other spheres also in which the puppets have an advantage over mere mortal actors. Fairy stories, legends of miraculous adventure, metamorphoses are tremendously heightened by the quality of strangeness inherent in the marionettes. "For puppet plays," says Professor Pischel, "are fairy-tales and the fairy-tale is nourished by strangeness." Transformations, animal fables, fairy flittings in scenes of mysterious glamour are obviously more easily presented by fleshless dolls than by heavy, panting and perspiring actors tricked out in unnatural and unearthly raiment.

Even horseplay humor of the Punch and Judy variety is unobjectionable with puppets where the whacking and thwacking is done by and upon jolly, grotesque little beings who are neither pained nor debased by the procedure. With some such idea William Hazlitt has written:

"That popular entertainment, Punch and the Puppet-show, owes part of its irresistible and universal attraction to nearly the same principle of inspiring inanimate and mechanical agents with sense and consciousness. The drollery and wit of a piece of wood

MARIONETTES

is doubly droll and farcical. Punch is not merry in himself, but 'he is the cause of heartfelt mirth in other men.' The wires and pulleys that govern his motion are conductors to carry off the spleen, and all 'that perilous stuff that weighs upon the heart.' If we see numbers of people turning the corner of a street, ready to burst with secret satisfaction, and with their faces bathed in laughter we know what is the matter — that they are just come from a puppet-show.

"I have heard no bad judge of such matters say that 'he liked a comedy better than a tragedy, a farce better than a comedy, a pantomime better than a farce, but a peep-show best of all.' I look upon it that he who invented puppet shows was a greater benefactor to his species than he who invented Operas!"

The marionette has come to America. Some of the more venturesome of this wandering race have crossed the high seas and entered hopefully into our open country. Are we not to welcome these immigrants? Can we not possibly assimilate them into our national life? Might we not benefit by their contribution? I make a plea for Polichinelle in the United States, the pleasant hours, the joyous moments of his bestowing.

How excellent if schools and playrooms might have their puppet booths for the happier exposition of folk and fairy tales or even for patriotic propaganda! I can see innumerable quaint silhouettes of *Pilgrim Fathers* bending the knee and giving thanks, or of *Indian Chiefs*, all feathery, in solemn conclave, with

Pocahontas dashing madly forward to save the life of Captain John Smith. It would be delicious to witness *George Washington*, in shadows, chopping down his father's little cherry tree: and as for *Lincoln and Slavery* . . . it actually happened that in 1867 Benedict Rivoli produced *Uncle Tom's Cabin*, with a company of puppets; it has happened in our vaudeville houses often, why not once in a while in our schools? Small groups of grown folks, too, in city or village, might easily build their own marionette stages and attempt to produce dramas of all times; humorous, satirical, poetic or mystical, each to his taste and independent of the whim of a Broadway manager or the peculiarities of a popular star. It is such a naïve and simple pastime and sometimes so delightful. I should like to suggest it as an antidote for the overdose of moving pictures from which an overwhelming number of us are unconsciously suffering atrophy of the imagination, or a similar insidious malady.[1]

[1] Mr. G. Bernard Shaw has written of England: "The old professional marionette showmen have been driven off the road by the picture theatre. I am told that on the Continent where marionettes flourish much more than here, they have suffered the same way from the competition of the irresistible pictures. And I doubt whether they will recover from the attack. I am afraid there is no use pretending that they deserve to."

How consoling to turn to Mr. Gordon Craig, who has prophesied optimistically in *The Marionette:* "Burattini are magical, whereas Cinema is only mechanical. When a frame-work of a film machine is one day found by curiosity-hunters in the ruins of a cellar and marvelled over, the Burattini will still be alive and kicking."

MARIONETTES

One must be quite unsophisticated to enjoy the marionettes, or quite sophisticated. Plain people, children and artists, seem to take pleasure in them. One must have something childlike, or artistic, in one's nature, perhaps merely a little imagination in an unspoiled, vigorous condition. Of course the stiff little figures, the peculiar conventions of the puppet stage are strange to us in America. There are those who do not *like* puppets and those who *do* not *can* not, I suppose. No one *must* like them: but none should scorn them. To scorn them is, somehow, to show too great disregard and lack of knowledge. And we, over here, who have not as youngsters laughed aloud at the drolleries of Guignol, who have not learned our folk-tales interspersed with the antics of some local Kasperle, who are not surprised by Punch and Judy at a familiar street corner, now and then, who have not been privileged to witness the spectacular faeries of Italian fantoccini, the exquisite shadows of the Chat Noir, the elaborate modern plays at the Munich art-theatre, — how can we really say *what* we think of the marionette? If we see more of him first; if we give our puppeteers (professional and amateur) more time to master their craft, perhaps, who knows, something nice may come of it all. There are some great words I should like to quote for little Polichinelle, artificial or strange as he may seem. "And therefore, as a stranger, give him welcome."

Behind the Scenes

FOR THE FUN OF IT

BUT why prate of benefit or pleasure to past or present audiences of the marionette when the best reason for the pupazzi, the true reason I do believe, for their continuance and longevity is the *fun* of puppet-playing? I confess it: nay, I proclaim it the foundation for my deep affection. And who shall find a firmer basis for any love than this, — interest, amusement, stimulation? Reverence or even understanding are far less vital, less compelling motives. Of course this applies to puppets. Everything applicable to humanity fits the burattini, for we are all so much the dancing dolls of destiny, satiric or serious, crude or precious puppets, all of us. One should truly have a fellow feeling for Punch and Judy.

As to the fun, however, of making puppets and of tinkering with the mechanical contrivances, the total absorption with such problems and the elation in overcoming absurd but seemingly insurmountable technical difficulties; the delight in carving and cutting, in designing costumes and then in sewing, glueing, painting, patching them into proper semblance of the original design: the art required properly to conceive a setting for dolls, the ingenuity exerted to decorate the stage, the delicious Lilliputian proportions of things, the charming effects contrived out of almost anything or nothing at all; and, in manipulating, the thrill of acquiring after long effort a full control of the doll at the end of the wires, of telegraphing one's emotions down into the responsive little body; and the whimiscal delight in writing for puppets (one dare be so impudent, being so impersonal and unpretentious!) — who shall say that such an aggregate of wholesome, creative enjoyment to an entire group of childlike grown-up folk is not sufficient vindication for Polichinelle and his kind? With so much bubbling enthusiasm behind the scenes, how can a proper audience be altogether bored? If they are bored it is a sure sign they are no proper audience!

WRITING FOR THE PUPPETS

"The life of man to represent
And turn it all to ridicule,
Wit did a puppet-show invent,
Where the chief actor is a fool."
—JONATHAN SWIFT.

No one appreciates how funny people are until he has written a play for puppets. There's nothing any person has ever said which isn't amusing, honestly and truly amusing, when transferred to the mouth of a marionette. Try it and see.

Take any conversation you may have overheard. Take as many puppets as there were people talking. Dress them to indicate the characters, try to imitate the most pronounced gestures and postures of your people. . . . and let them speak, verbatim, the words that have been spoken.

It is simply funny, a sort of unconscious, undeniable criticism of the manners of men. There will always be a *point*, too, a sort of moral at the minimum. No one can fail to see it, either in the words or the gestures or the situations. The puppets will find it and bring it out. Produce the puppets and try it!

I frankly confess I shudder to imagine myself *done in puppet*. What a cure for idiosyncrasies and affectations!

A REHEARSAL OF TINTAGILES

In all the lack-luster of realism we "stood on the bridge at midnight." Four of us stood on the bridge and we were very weary. It was the bridge of our marionette stage over which we had been bending for hours. From out in front somewhere the director spoke: "Now, once more the third act . . . and remember they must lean *against* the door when it opens as if they were trying desperately to hold it. See that the strings do not catch. Readers, please watch the figures and give them plenty of time. . . . Ready?" We were, tensely so.

The beautiful, sad voice of Ygraine gave us the mood. "I have been to look at the doors . . . there are three of them. . . ." Aglovale (old and tremulous): "I will go seat myself upon the step, my sword upon my knee. . . ."

MARIONETTES

"Aglovale, lean back farther against the step; don't perch on the edge." (This from the front.) Aggie (as we familiarly called him) thereupon proceeded to jerk up and sit down deliberately a couple of times, then followed a twitching, collapsing, stiffening process. . . . "Sorry, it's the little hump in his shoulders and the step is so narrow!" wailed a tired unseen operator. During the struggle Belangere flopped inelegantly on the floor, her manipulator resting a weary wrist. Clearing of throats, scraping of chairs from the readers in the wings.

Patient director: "Well, let it go for to-night. You may have to remove the hump. Are we ready?" We were.

The play proceeded. On the miniature stage in dim, high-arched rooms, bare and gloomy, slender, strange little creatures moved with stiff, imposing gestures. It is an ominous world, the atmosphere vibrating with hidden terror, tense emotions and lonely overtones. Princess Ygraine, to the little Tintagiles: "There, you see . . . ? Your big sisters are here . . . they are close to you . . . we will defend you and no evil can come near."

Oh, the tenderness, the dauntlessness, the pathos . . . high hearts encircled by creeping, inevitable doom.

Then the old man, mumbling at his own bewildered futility: "My soul is heavy to-day." (A hand is raised, an old hand, tremblingly.) "What is one to do . . . ? Men needs must live and await the unforeseen. . . . And after that they must still act as if they hoped. . . ." (The arm drops, heavy . . . a silence.) "There are sad evenings when our useless lives taste bitter in our mouths . . . etc."

The scene proceeds, on and on in ascending tensity, readers sitting at the wings, puppeteers operating the wires high up, the director off at his desk in the dark, . . . and the marionettes animated into vital significance, symbols of supreme and simplified fervor . . . dread, love, courage. . . .

"They are shaking the door, listen. Do not breathe. They are whispering.

"They have the key . . .

"Yes, yes, I was sure of it. . . . Wait. . . ."

Old Aglovale faces the slowly opening door, his sword outstretched; the others stand rigid with terror.

"Come! Come both. . . ."

They face the door, they hold it. Their watchfulness avails for the time being. The door closes.

"Tintagiles!"

Aglovale, waiting at the door: "I hear nothing now. . . ."

Ygraine, wild with joy. "Tintagiles, look! Look! . . . He is saved! . . . Look at his eyes. . . . You can see the blue. . . . He is going to speak. . . . They saw we were watching. . . . They did not dare. . . . Kiss us! . . . Kiss us, I say! . . . All, all! . . . Down to the depths of our soul! . . ."

A silence, a long silence. Then . . . the boards

creak as the operators stand up to rest their aching backs.

"Well, Belangere mounted the steps pretty well that time. But don't forget to take a stitch in her left leg; she still has a tendency to pivot."

"Yes, I'll do it and I'll lengthen her back string; I think that's it . . . and take away some of Aggie's hump."

From the sublime to the absurd, no doubt. But there are the puppets hung up . . . quietly and sternly gazing, each little character.

No, they are not absurd, patiently, almost scornfully awaiting the subtler grasp of some master hand to bring out the rare potentialities sleeping within them. Awkward, silly dolls they may appear in a clumsy hand, but even we amateurs who serve them faithfully sense more than this in them. So, while we pull the strings and move these singular, small creatures in measured gestures we feel that we are handling crude but expressive symbols of large, fine things.

THE MAKING OF A MARIONETTE

The puppets used in the Cleveland Playhouse are neither realistic, humorous, nor clever. They are very simple, somewhat impressionistic and quite adequate and effective for certain types of drama. They appeal to the imagination of the spectator. Under favorable conditions one forgets their diminutive size, their crude construction, even their lack of soul.

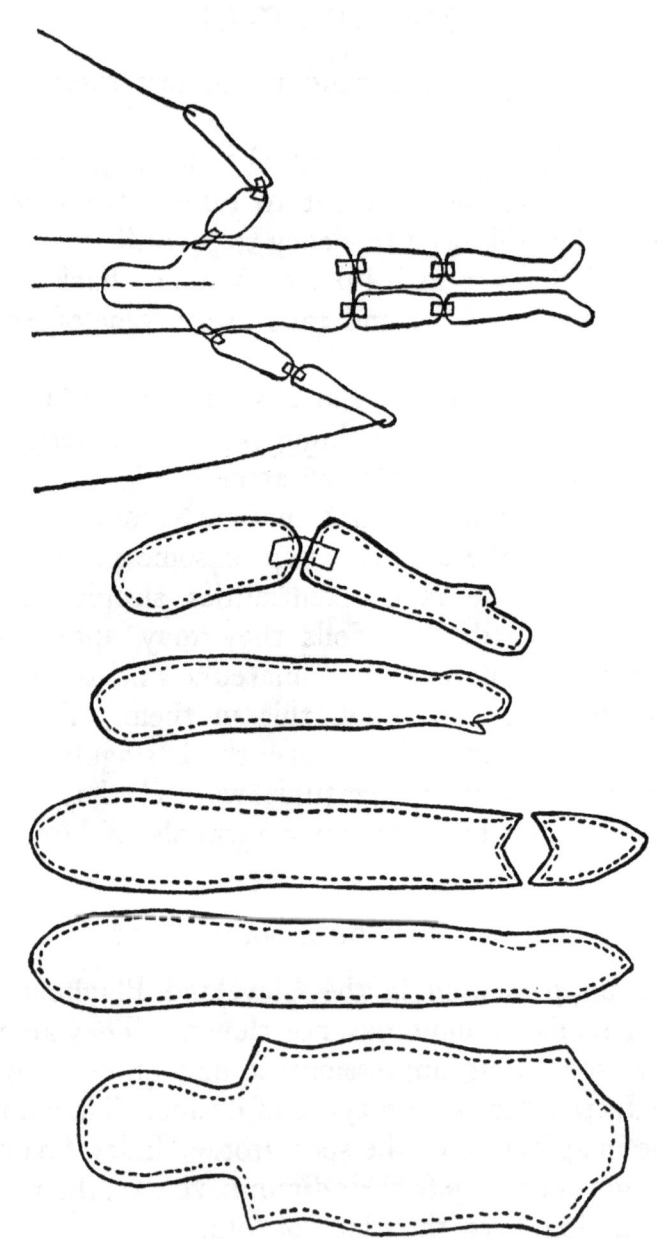

Patterns for the Marionette Body drawn by the Sculptor, Mr. Max Kalish

MARIONETTES

These patterns for the marionette body were drawn by the sculptor, Mr. Max Kalish, especially for figures which were shown with little clothing on. If the dolls are to be dressed it is better to make separate upper and lower arms and legs, and to join them flexibly or stiffly, as the action of the particular puppet requires.

The material we have used is soft white woven stuff (stockings from the ten-cent store!), which can be painted with tempera any color desired. The patterns shown allow for a good seam. The front and back are alike, also right and left limbs. Each marionette will need some adjusting which one discovers as one works along. We have used a narrow tape to join the arms and legs.

The dolls are stuffed with soft rags or cotton. The limbs must be stiffly filled out and firm, the chest also. The lower part of the torso should be left softer. In the hands we insert cardboard to stiffen the wrists.

We use lead to weight the dolls. Small shot is good for filling up the hands and feet. Larger pieces of lead are used for the torso, lower arm and lower leg. No lead is put in the upper arm or upper leg. The reasons for this will be discovered as soon as one practices manipulating the figures. Care must be used to have the body properly balanced and to have the feet heavy.

The control is a simple piece of wood with five screw eyes to which the strings are tied. More may be added to operate the feet or for other purposes.

When using these extremely crude little dolls, however, it is best to depend upon simple means and a few gestures. The strings can be of heavy black thread or fishing cord, the latter is not so apt to become twisted. The strings are attached to the hands, the shoulders, and the center of the back. The hand strings should be loose, the others carefully measured to balance the doll evenly.

In dressing the puppets one must allow plenty of room at the elbow, knee, etc., for free action. We have kept our dolls very simple, the faces and hands painted over, the hair of wool or cotton.

Of the manipulating little can be said. There is no way to learn except by getting up on the bridge and *doing* it. Too much petty gesticulation in these dolls is ineffective. It is better to hold the gesture. Deliberation and patience are the chief requirements for a successful operator, given a certain natural deftness of hand which is primarily essential.

Construction of a Marionette Stage

By Raymond O'Neil

The marionette stage shown in the diagram has a proscenium opening six feet long by four feet high and is meant for productions that use marionettes from twelve to fourteen inches in height. It is a stage that can be built even by amateurs both readily and cheaply. It is, of course, necessary that some one who is familiar with the electric wiring should be consulted in that part of the work.

The stage is in two sections: the stage floor proper, to which is attached the footlight box, and the proscenium arch, which is made to be demounted and is held to the stage floor by right angle braces. The stage floor itself is made of $\frac{7}{8}''$ stock which may run from eight to twelve inches in width. These boards are fastened to 2 x 4's which run from the front to the back of the stage. Three lengths of these 2 x 4's are all that are necessary. The box which holds the footlights may be made of $\frac{1}{2}''$ stock which should be just deep enough to hold 60-watt lamps. Three circuits should be run into this box to provide for red, blue and green lamps. The diagram shows only one lamp to each color placed in the box, but to obtain the best results three or four lamps should be used on each circuit. Small stage connectors which can be obtained at any electrical dealer's should be placed in the floor to take care of the lines that run to No. 1 border, No. 2 border and to the various other lamps such as small floods and small spotlights, which will be found necessary for different effects. Both No. 1 and No. 2 borders should have three circuits running into them for red, blue and green lamps, and there should be from four to six lamps on each circuit. These borders may be placed in any position from the front to the back of the stage that the setting may demand. A convenient place from which to suspend them is from the operating platform which is built over the complete length of the stage at such a height as to clear any set that may be used.

The proscenium arch should be built of $\frac{7}{8}''$ stock, preferably of white wood, because of the fine surface which it presents, if it is to be decorated. The upright sections of the arch should be at least as wide as those shown in the diagram, because they must carry the three circuits for the proscenium lights, the belt that raises and lowers the curtain, and also special lamps and appliances that will be found necessary for various types of production. The diagram shows one green, one blue, and one red outlet on the two sections on the top section of the arch, but it will be found very convenient to have at least two outlets for each of these colors on each of the three sections of the arch.

The curtain can be the ordinary window shade.

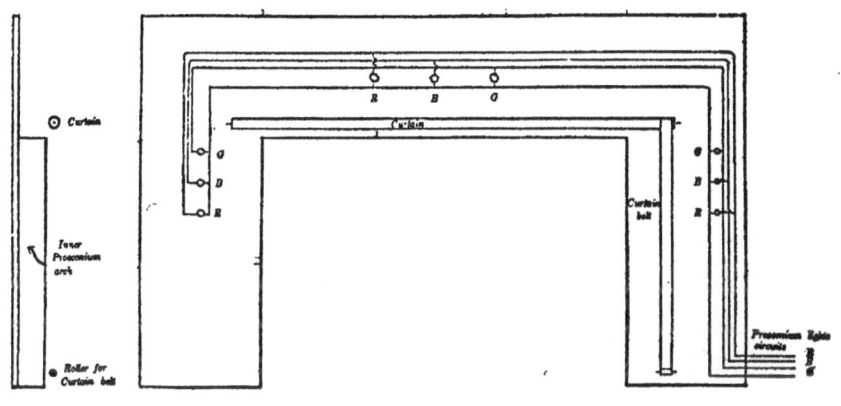

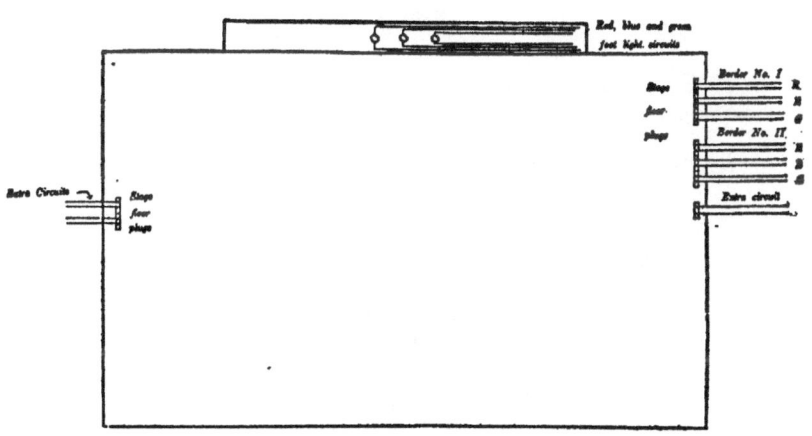

DIAGRAMS FOR THE CONSTRUCTION OF A MARIONETTE STAGE

MARIONETTES

After removing the spring, attach it to the face of the proscenium arch with ordinary window shade fixtures. It should be wide enough to lap well over each side of the arch, and the end which extends to the right of the proscenium opening should be sufficiently long to carry a 2" belt for raising and lowering it. This belt can be of webbing and should be held taut near the bottom of the proscenium arch by a small roller, as shown in the diagram. It is necessary that this belt should be far enough to the right of the proscenium arch opening so the hand which raises and lowers the curtain will not be seen by the audience.

The outlets for the various circuits on this arch may be either keyed sockets or porcelain receptacles fastened to the face of the arch.

Both for the sake of the better framing of the settings to be used on this stage and for more effectively masking off the sides and the top of the stage, it is a good plan to build all around the opening of the proscenium arch at right angles to it an inner proscenium which may run from 6 to 9 inches in width. This inner proscenium may be made of half-inch stock. If the inner proscenium is used, it will be necessary to hang the curtain sufficiently behind the face of the main proscenium so that it will clear the inner proscenium as it rises and falls.

All circuits should lead to a switch-board on which small knife switches may be used. This switch-board should also carry several rheostats or dimmers. The more dimmers that are used the greater will be the possibilities in lighting. These dimmers can be made of special high wattage resistance wire, which can be obtained or ordered from any electrical dealer. In the making and wiring of the switch-board, it is, of course, necessary to obtain either a professional electrician or at least professional advice.

BIBLIOGRAPHY

BADIN, ADOLPHE. Les Marionettes de Maurice Sand. L'Art, 1885.
CAINE, WILLIAM. Guignols in the Luxembourg. Oxford and Cambridge Review, 1910.
CALTHROP, A. An Evening with the Marionette. The Theatre, 1884.
CALVI, EMILIO. Marionettes of Rome. The Bellman, 1917.
CHAMBERS, E. K. The Mediaeval Stage. Vol. II.
COLLIER, JOHN PAYNE. The Tragical Comedy of Punch and Judy.
CRAIG, GORDON. Articles in "The Mask" and "The Marionette."
CURTIS, ELNORA WHITMAN. Dramatic Instinct in Education.
DELVAU, ALFRED. Le Théâtre Érotique Français sous le Bas-empire.
DURANTY, LOUIS ÉMILE EDMOND. Théâtre des Marionettes du Jardin des Tuileries.
ENGEL, CARL. Johann Faust.
FEISE, E. The German Puppet Theatre.
FERRIGNI, P. Storia dei Burattini. The Mask.
FEWKES, JESSE WALTER. A Theatrical Performance at Walpe. Hopi Katchinas.
FLÖGEL, KARL FRIEDERICH. Geschichte des Grotesk-Komischen.
FRANCE, ANATOLE. On Life and Letters. II Series.

GAYET, A. Oldest of Puppet Shows. Boston Transcript, Nov. 2, 1904.
GLEASON, A. W. Last Stand of the Marionettes. Collier's Weekly, 1909.
HIRSCH, GILBERT. A Master of Marionettes. Harper's Weekly, 1912.
IRWIN, E. Where Players are Marionettes. The Craftsman, 1907.
JACKSON, F. NEVILL. Toys of Other Days.
JACOB, GEORG. Das Schattentheater in seiner Wanderung vom Morgenland zum Abendland.
JEROME, L. B. Marionettes of Little Sicily. New England Magazine, 1910.
JOLY, HENRI L. Random Notes on Dances, Masks, and the Early Forms of Theatre in Japan.
JONES, HENRY FESTING. Diversions in Sicily, Castellinaria, or other Sicilian Diversions.
KLEIST, HEINRICH VON. Über das Marionetten Theater. Berliner Abendblätter.
KOLLMAN, ARTHUR. Deutsche Puppenspieler.
LEE, VERNON. Studies in the Eighteenth Century in Italy.
LEMAÎTRE, JULES. Impressions du Théâtre. Vols. IV and VI.
MACDOWALL, H. C. The Faust of the Marionettes. MacMillan's Magazine, 1901.
MAGNIN, CHARLES. Histoire des Marionettes en Europe.
MAINDRON, ERNEST. Marionettes et Guignols.
MATTHEWS, BRANDER. A Book about the Theatre. Puppet plays, old and new. The Bookman.
MICHEL, WILHELM. Marionetten. Dekorative Kunst, 1910.
MICK, HETTIE LOUISE. Puppets of the Chicago Little Theatre. Theatre Arts Magazine, 1917.

BIBLIOGRAPHY 231

MIYAMORI, OSATARO. Tales from Old Japanese Drama.
MODERWELL, HIRAM K. The Marionettes of Tony Sarg. Boston Transcript, 1918.
MOULTON, R. H. Teaching Dolls to act for Moving Pictures. Illustrated World, 1917.
NICHOLS, FRANCIS H. A Marionette Theatre in New York. Century Magazine, 1892.
PEIXOTTO, ERNEST C. Marionettes, and Puppet Shows, Past and Present. Scribner's Magazine, 1903.
PETITE, J. M. Guignols et Marionettes.
PISCHEL, RICHARD. The Home of the Puppet Play. (Translated by Mildred C. Tawney.)
POCCI, FRANZ VON. Lustiges Komödienbüchlein.
POLLOCK, W. H. Punch and Judy. Saturday Review, 1900.
REHM, HERMANN SIEGFRIED. Das Buch der Marionetten.
SERRURIER, L. De Wajang Poerwa.
SERVAES, FRANZ. Neue Theaterpuppen von R. Teschner.
SPERANZA, GINO CHARLES. Marionette Theatre in New York. Saturday Evening Post, 1916.
STARR, LAURA B. The Doll Book.
STEVENSON, ROBERT LOUIS. Essays.
STODDARD, ANNE. The Renaissance of the Puppet Play. Century Magazine, 1918.
STORM, THEODOR. Pole Poppenspäler.
STRUTT, JOSEPH. Sports and Pastimes of the People of England.
SYMONS, H. An Apology for Puppets. Saturday Review, 1897.
VASARI. Life of Il Cecca.
VISAN, TANCRÈDE DE. Le Théâtre de Guignol. Nouvelle Revue, 1909.

BIBLIOGRAPHY

WEED, INIS. Puppet Plays for Children. Century Magazine, 1916.
WEST, HENRY SUYDAM. Puppet Warfare in France. Literary Digest, 1915.
WESTWOOD, J. O. Notice of Medieval Mimic Entertainment. Archeological Journal, Vol. V.
WITKOWSKI, GEORG. Introduction to Goethe's Faust.
WOLF, GEORG JACOB. Das Marionetten Theater Münchner Künstler. Dekorative Kunst, 1911.
YOUNG, S. G. Guignol. Lippincott's Magazine, 1879.
ZIEGLER, FRANCIS J. Puppets, Ancient and Modern. Harper's Magazine, 1897.

All the Year, 1894. Greek Puppet Show. From the Works of Heron of Alexandria.
Current Opinion, 1916. Paradox of the Puppet.
Current Opinion, 1913. Return of the Marionettes.
Eclectic Magazine, 1854. Puppets of All Nations.
Encyclopaedia Britannica, Vol. 17: 723.
Illustrated London News, 1911. A Javanese Topeng Dalang.
Kind und Kunst. Vol. III. Illustrations of Puppet Shows.
Scientific American, 1902. Puppet Shows of the Paris Exposition.
The Marionette. Vol. I.
The Mask. Vols. I, II, III, IV, V, VI, VII.
The Sketch, 1916. Illustration of the Gair Wilkinsons' Puppets.

Index

Ache, d', Caran, designs silhouettes for *Chat Noir*, 98–99.
Actors, used with marionettes, in Italian church festivals, 51; in medieval French churches, 82; in Germany in seventeenth century, 123–125.
Aiken, Vivian, 183.
Alice in Wonderland, in Chicago, 178.
America, marionettes in, 163–191.
American Indians, use of articulated images in ceremonials, 164–170.
Ames, Winthrop, interest in marionettes, 184–185.
Ananda, annual performance in temple, 30.
Anatole, M., founder of the Vrai Guignol, 107–108.
Antinoe, excavation of marionette theatre in, 16–17.
Antiquity of puppets, 15.
Antwerp, underground theatre in, 141–142.
Apotheosis of Bacchus, representative Greek show, 19.
Apuleius, quoted on Greek puppets, 18.
Ariosto's *Orlando Furioso* in Sicily, 71–76.
Aristophanes' *The Birds* in puppet performance, 105.
Arlecchino, Italian puppet character, 22, 57.

Baden-Baden, puppet show of Ivo Pühony, 134.

Bali, Wayang plays in, 28.
Belgium, puppets in, 140–142.
Bergerac, Cyrano de, duel with ape, 84.
Berlin, production of *Doctor Sassafras* and *Two Dancing Chinamen*, 134–135.
Bertrand, French showman, 86–87.
Birds of Aristophanes produced, 105.
Black, John, 182
Blei, Franz, quoted on shadow play in Munich, 132; on types of plays for puppets, 210–211.
Bohemia, puppet plays in, 136.
Boinet, Paul, operator on *La France*, 109.
Bologna, theatres in, 69.
Bonifrates, definition, 80.
Boswell, quoted, 154.
Bouchor, Maurice, presents *Noël ou le Mystère de la Nativité*, 110–111.
Brann, Paul, founder of theatre in Munich, 130.
Briocci. *See* Brioché.
Brioché, Giovanni and Francesco, famous 17th century showmen, 84–86.
Broemel, Carl, 183.
Browne, Mrs. Maurice, founder of Chicago Little Theatre, 173–178.
Bue ens, Pieter, Belgian showman, 141.
Buffano, Remo, 171.
Bulley, Margaret, 157.
Burattini, description, 54; derivation of name, 55.
Burma, development of puppet stage, 29–30.

CAINE, W., quoted on Paris Guignols, 197–198.
Calthrop, A., on modern Venetian show, 68.
Cardboard plays, 192–194.
Cascio, Salvatore, 172.
Cassandrino, Italian puppet character, 58, 60.
Catacombs, jointed images in tombs, 22.
Catania, religious plays in, 77–78.
Cecca, mediæval Italian mechanician, 51–52.
Central Asia, two types of puppets, 30.
Ceylon, early religious puppets, 33.
Chambers, E. K., quoted on use of puppets in churches, 53.
Champs Élysées, home of the Vrai Guignol, 107–108; performances, 197–198.
Character types. *See* Types.
Charles V of Spain, 78.
Chat Noir, home of *Ombres Françaises*, 98–100.
Chicago Little Theatre, successful performances in, 173–178.
Children's productions, 192–194.
Chopin, life enacted by Cleveland puppets, 182.
Christmas plays. *See* Religious plays.
Church festivals, in Italy, 51–52. *See also* Passion play; Religious plays.
Cibber, Colley, writes for marionettes, 153.
Cleveland, Italian performance in, 172; Playhouse, puppet productions, 178–183; performance of *The Rose and the Ring*, 200–201; construction of dolls, 221–224.
Clisby, George, 179.
Cologne, home of Kölner Hanneschen Theatre, 128.

Comic element in puppets, 203–205.
Commedia dell'arte, influence on Italian marionettes, 57–59.
Constantine, Italian puppet character, 58.
Construction of marionettes, 221–224. *See also* Materials; Mechanism.
Construction of marionette stage (O'Neil), 226–229.
Craig, Gordon, experiments with puppets, 160–163; *Game of Marionettes*, 192; on educational importance of puppets, 202; on actor and marionette, 208–209; on future of puppet plays, 214.
Crawley, London showman, 153.
Cruikshank, pictures of Punch and Judy, 149.
Cuccoli, Filippo, 69.
Curtis, Elnora Whitman, on educational value of puppets, 201–202.

DALANG, definition, 27.
Dame aux Camellias (*La*), parody on by George Sand, 94.
Death of Tintagiles, production in Cleveland, 179–180; rehearsal of, 218–221.
Deaves, Harry, retired American marionettist, 171.
Deluded Dragon, produced at Chicago Little Theatre, 174–175.
Denmark, puppets in literature, 140.
Dickens, Charles, quoted on puppet shows in Genoa, 63–66.
Dickson (pseud.), operator-magician, 101.
Dieppe, annual *Mystery of the Assumption*, 82–83.
Docha, definition, 113.
Doctor Sassafras, artistic production in Berlin, 134–135.

INDEX 235

Dolls, mechanical, in vaudeville, 170–171.
Domèvre, *The Seven Chasseurs of*, 111–112.
Don Quixote and the puppets, 79.
Dorothea, popular puppet character of Hamburg, 115.
Drama, poetic, difficulties of production, 190–191. *See also* Plays.
Drama, varied repertory of Italian marionettes, 59–62; classic, given at *Le Petit Théâtre de M. Henri Signoret*, 102–105.
Duranty, Charles, attempt to uplift Guignol, 108.

EDGERTON, Mrs. Seymour, 174.
Educational value of puppets, 195, 201–202, 213–214.
Egypt, possible birth-place of marionettes, 16.
Ehlert, Ernest, gives shows in Berlin with Pühony's puppets, 134–135; on Pühony's marionettes, 206.
Elizabethan period, popularity of puppets, 150–154.
England, puppets in, 143–163; toy theatres in, 193–194.
English literature full of allusions to puppets, 143–144.
Epopée, produced at *Chat Noir*, 99.
Erotikon Theatron de la rue de la Santé, sketch of, 94–96.
Eudel, Paul, first publishes shadow plays, 98.
Excavations reveal ancient puppets, 16–17.

FAIRY plays, in the *Ombres Chinoises* at Versailles, 97–98; in the *Vrai Guignol*, 108; in Munich, 129; at Chicago Little Theatre, 174–178; produced by Tony Sarg, 186–187, 189; specially suited to puppets, 212.
Fantoccini, description, 54; derivation of name, 55.
Fashion puppet, Lady Jane, 152.
Faust, history of character, 116–122.
Ferrigni, P., on introduction of figures into Christian churches, 23. *See also* Yorick.
Fewkes, Dr. Jesse Walter, quoted on Indian ceremonial drama, 164–170.
Fiano Theatre, Rome, 60–61.
Figurini, derivation of name, 55.
Flögel, quoted on English masques, 145–146; preference for grotesque comedy, 203.
France, Anatole, writes on the *Chat Noir*, 98; quoted on *Le Petit Théâtre de M. Henri Signoret*, 103–105.
France, puppets in, 81–112.
Francisque, French showman introducing *opéra comique*, 88–89.
French writers and musicians, show interest in puppets, 89–96.
Fun in puppet-playing, 216–218.

GAUTIER, Théophile, on Turkish puppets, 37.
Gayet, A., on puppet theatre excavated at Antinoë, 16–17.
Gehring, Albert, 182.
Geisselbrecht, Viennese showman, 121.
Genoa, elaborate productions in, 62–66.
Germany, puppet shows in, 113–136; toy theatres in, 194–196.
Gidayu, definition, 46.
Gidayu, Takemoto, 16th century showman, 47–48.
Glasheimer, Adolf, Berlin showman, 126.

INDEX

Gleason, Arthur, describes Italian show in New York, 172–173.
Goethe, interest in puppets, 122; maxim on stagecraft, 161; quoted on his introduction to puppets, 195–196.
Golden age of marionettes, 89.
Goldoni, interest in puppets, 197.
Goldsmith, Oliver, at marionette show, 154.
Grasso, Maria, 172.
Greece, articulated idols in, 17; development of puppetry in, 18–21.
"Green monster" of George Sand, 93.
Grotesqueness in puppets, 203.
Guignol, originated in Lyons, 107; in Paris, 107–108; on steamship *La France*, 109; performances in Paris, 197–198.
Gyp, presents *Tout à l'égout*, 110.

HAMBURG, long popularity of puppets in, 115–116.
Hanswurst, German puppet buffoon, 114.
Hauptundstaatsactionen, description of, 124–125.
Haydn, Joseph, composes music for marionettes, 127.
Hazlitt, William, on Punch and Judy shows, 212–213.
Hembauf, George, Belgian showman, 140.
Heron of Alexandria, on early Greek puppet mechanism, 19.
Hewelt, John (pseud.), operator-magician, 101.
Holden, Thomas, operator-magician, 101; marionettes, 156.
Holland, puppets in, 140.
Hopi Indians, Great Serpent drama, 165–170.

Humor in puppet plays, 203–205.
Hungary, gypsy puppeteers, 136.

IDOLS, animated, in Egypt, 16; in Greece, 18; in Rome, 21; of ancient Gauls, 81. *See also* Images; Religious puppets; Statues.
Ilkely Players, amateur English marionettists, 157.
Images, jointed, found in Catacombs, 22; religious, in Italy, 51–54; articulated, used in mediæval French churches, 81–82; in English churches, 145; articulated, used by American Indians, 164–170. *See also* Idols; Religious puppets; Statues.
India, antiquity of puppets, 15; development of puppets in, 32–35.
Israeli, d', Isaac, writes of Punch, 146–147.
Italy, evolution of puppetry, 22; its development, 50–78; Goldoni's interest in puppets, 197; puppets beloved by children, 199–200.

JAPAN, origin and development of puppet shows, 43–49.
Java, shadow-plays, 24–28.
Jinavaravamsa, P. C., on Indian puppets to-day, 34.
Joly, Henri, on antiquity of Japanese shows, 43–44.
Jones, Henry Festing, quoted on Sicilian shows, 71–77.
Jonson, Ben, mentions puppets in many writings, 150–151.
Joruri, Japanese epic play, 47.
Juvenile drama, 193–194.

KARAGHEUZ, Turkish puppet hero, 37.
Kasperle, German puppet buffoon, 114; in Faust play, 118–120.

INDEX

Ketschel, Persian comic puppet, 32.
Kobold, definition, 113.
Kölner Hanneschen Theater, 128.
Kopecki, Bohemian showman, 136.
Kreymborg, Alfred, 183.
LA FRANCE, puppet theatre on, 109.
La Grille's *Théâtre des Pygmées*, 87–88.
Laufer, Dr. Berthold, on marionettes in Egypt, 16.
Laurent Broeders, Belgian showmen, 140–141.
Lemaître, Jules, describes several productions, 110–111.
Lewiss, Clunn, wandering English showman, 155–156.
Lighting a puppet stage, 227–229.
Lima Beans, given in Los Angeles, 183.
Literary puppets in Paris, 109–111.
Little Theatre, Chicago, history of, 173–178.
London, Italian puppets in, 146; present-day street puppets, 155.
Los Angeles, puppets in, 183.
Louis XIV, puppets a feature of marriage procession, 79; gives special privileges to La Grille, 88.
Lupi brothers, Italian showmen, 68–69; description of performance for children, 199–200.
Luschan, von, F., on puppet plays in Turkey, 38.
Luther, Martin, denunciations against actors, 123.

MACCUS, Roman buffoon, 21.
Machieltje, Belgian showman, 140.
MacLean, J. Arthur, on puppet performance at Ananda, 29–30.

Maeterlinck's *Death of Tintagiles* produced in Cleveland, 179–180; rehearsal of play, 218–221.
Magnin, Charles, on Greek articulated idols, 18; on Polichinelle, 205.
Mahabharata, basis of Javanese plays, 26.
Making a marionette, 221–224. *See also* Materials; Mechanism.
Manik Muja, basis of Javanese plays, 26.
Margueritte, Paul, describes M. Signoret's puppets, 207.
Marionette, derivation of name, 55.
Marionette Theatre of Munich Artists, 130–131.
Masques, English, 145–146.
Materials, used in ancient Indian puppets, 15; in Javanese shadows, 25; in Siamese shadows, 29; in Cleveland Playhouse puppets, 179–180; making a marionette to-day, 221–224.
Matthews, Brander, on types of plays for puppets, 211–212.
Maupassant, de, Guy, on Karagheuz plays, 39.
Mechanical dolls in vaudeville, 170–171.
Mechanism, of early Greek puppets, 18; of Javanese shadows, 27; of modern Indian puppets, 34; of Turkish puppets, 38; intricacy of in Japanese puppets, 45–46; of Italian puppets, 54–55; intricate, in modern Italian puppets, 70; increasing intricacy in France, 90; of *Le Petit Théâtre de M. Henri Signoret*, 102–103; perfection in Tony Sarg's puppets, 185–186; simple, in Cleveland Playhouse dolls, 221–224.
Michel, Wilhelm, on comic function of puppets, 204.

INDEX

Mick, Hettie Louise, writes on plays at Chicago Little Theatre, 175-176.
Midsummer Night's Dream, production at Chicago Little Theatre, 175-177.
Molière's *Monsieur Pourceaugnac* in Madrid, 80.
Monzayemon, Chikamatsu, Japanese playwright, 48.
Mourguet, Laurent, originator of Guignol, 107.
Munich, home of best German puppet shows, 128-133.
Musée Grevin, theatre in, 109.

NANG, Siamese shadow play, 28-29.
Nantes, revocation of Edict made into play, 86-87.
Napoleon, death of, puppet play described by Dickens, 64-66.
Nelson, Lord, imaginary dialogue with Punch, 149.
Neuville, de, Lemercier, guiding spirit of *Erotikon Theatron*, 95-96; interest in shadow plays, 98.
New York, Italian show described by Arthur Gleason, 172-173; puppets of Tony Sarg, 183-191.
Noël, by Bouchor, 110-111.

OGOTAI, legend of, 31.
Ombres Chinoises, French shadow plays, 97.
Ombres Françaises, at the *Chat Noir* 98-100.
Ombre du cocher poète, L', first *opéra comique*, 88-89.
O'Neil, Raymond, director Cleveland Playhouse, 178; "Construction of Marionette Stage," 226-229.
Opéra comique, origin, 88-89.
Operator-magicians, 101.

Origin of puppets, theories of scholars, 15-16; Persian legend, 31-32; Turkish tales, 36; Chinese legends, 40-41; Japanese stories, 44.
Orlando Furioso in Sicily, 71-76.
Osaka, puppet plays in, 48.
Owen, Lillian, 174.

PANDJI legends, basis of Javanese plays, 26.
Pantalone, Italian puppet character, 58.
Paris, first permanent puppet stage erected, 83; George Sand's theatre, 92-94; *Erotikon Theatron de la rue de la Santé*, 94-96; the *Chat Noir*, 98-100; the operator-magicians, 101; *Le Petit Théâtre de M. Henri Signoret*, 102-105; the *Vrai Guignol* in the Champs Élysées, 107-108; literary puppets, 109-111; marionette theatre at 1900 Exposition, 109; Guignol performances, 197-198.
Passion play, at Catania, 77-78.
Pathological types of Turkish puppets, 37.
Payne-Collier, arranges *Tragical Comedy of Punch and Judy*, 149.
Persia, puppetry in, 31-32.
Petit Théâtre in Belgium, 141.
Piccini, Italian showman in England, 146.
Pierrot Guitariste, puppet by De Neuville, 96.
Pinkethman, London showman, 153.
Pischel, Prof. Richard, on origin of puppets, 15-16; on puppet plays of India, 32-33.
Pivetta, definition, 67.
Playhouse, in Cleveland, gives puppet plays, 178-183; construction of dolls, 221-224.
Plays, suited to puppets, 210-214.

INDEX 239

Pocci, Graf, writer of fairy plays for puppets, 129; *Three Wishes* produced by Tony Sarg, 186–187.

Poetic drama, difficulties of production, 190–191.

Poland, religious plays in, 138–139; Wyspianski's interest in puppets, 196–197.

Polichinelle, French puppet character, 83; varied career, 106–107; plea for, 203–215. *See also* Pulcinella; Punch; Punchinello.

Pollock, B., publisher of juvenile plays, 193–194.

Portugal, puppets in, 80.

Powell, clever London motion maker, 151–152.

Prodigal Son, popular play in Hamburg, 115.

Producing a play, in Java, 26; in India, 34; in Turkey, 38; in China, 41–43; in Japan, 45–47; French restrictions in 17th century, 87–88; *Midsummer Night's Dream* in Chicago, 176–177; behind the scenes, 216–224; construction of stage, 226–229.

Pühony, Ivo, puppet maker, 134; his marionettes, Ernst Ehlert quoted, 206.

Pulcinella, Italian puppet character, 22, 58. *See also* Polichinelle; Punch; Punchinello.

Punch, origin of name, 146–147. *See also* Polichinelle; Pulcinella.

Punchinello, his prestige and prowess, 147–150. *See also* Polichinelle; Pulcinella; Punch.

Pupazzi, derivation of name, 55.

RAMAYANA, basis of Javanese plays, 26; basis of Siamese *Nang*, 28; modern production of in India, 34.

Rehearsal of play, 218–221.

Rehm, R. S., on puppet show in Samarkand, 30–31; on Chinese shadows, 42–43; on Rivière's shadow pantomimes, 99–100.

Religious plays, at Catania, 77–78; in Spain, 78; revocation of Edict of Nantes produced, 86–87; in Russia, 137–139; in Poland, 138–139; in England, 145; specially suited to marionettes, 211. *See also* Passion play.

Religious puppets, at Antinoë, 17; in Greece, 18; in Rome, 21; in Catacombs, 22; in Burma, 30; in Ceylon, 33. *See also* Idols; Images; Statues.

Repertory, varied in Italian puppet shows, 56–62; varied in medieval Germany, 123–125; in Munich theatres, 131–132.

Restrictions on production, in 17th century France, 87–88.

Rivière, Henri, makes pantomimes for *Chat Noir*, 99–100.

Rome, ancient, articulated statues, 21; Rome, modern, many puppet theatres in, 60–62.

Rose and the Ring produced by Tony Sarg, 189–190; account of Cleveland performance, 200–201.

Russia, puppet plays in, 137–139.

SAINT-GENOIS, de, Alfred and Charles, 101.

Saint Germain Fair, puppet shows at, 87.

Saint Laurent Fair, puppet shows at, 87.

Salome, in puppet performance, 211–212.

Samarkand, performance of *Tschadar Chajal* in, 30–31.

INDEX

Sand, George, establishes *Théâtre des Amis*, 92-94.
Sanskrit, restriction in use of, 33.
Sarg, Tony, experiments with marionettes in London and New York, 184-191; takes *The Rose and the Ring* to Cleveland, 200-201.
Scala, Flaminio, 17th century director, 59.
Scapino, Italian puppet character, 58.
Scaramuccia, Italian puppet character, 58.
Sceaux, puppet stage in chateau, 89-90.
Schmidt, "Papa," beloved Munich showman, 129-130; appreciation of work, 195.
Schutz and Dreher, showman of Berlin, 121.
Seneca, death of, shown in Valencia, 80.
Seraphin, Dominique, producer of shadow plays, 97.
Shadow plays, in France, 96-100; in Munich, 132.
"Shadows," Javanese, how made, 25; of Siamese *Nang*, 28-29; Turkish, origin and excellence of, 36-39; Chinese development, 39-43.
Shadowy Waters produced by Cleveland puppets, 182.
Shakespeare, *Tempest* produced by M. Signoret, 103-104; allusions to puppet shows, 143-144; *Midsummer Night's Dream* in Chicago, 175-177.
Shaw, G. Bernard, on marionettes and acting, 209; on future of puppet shows, 214.
Siam, unusual shadows of the *Nang*, 28-29.
Sicily, great popularity of marionettes in, 70-78.

Signoret, Henri, le Petit Théâtre de, 102-103; puppets described by Paul Margueritte, 207-208.
Simmonds, William, artist and amateur puppeteer, 158-160.
Simplification of puppets by Gordon Craig, 162-163.
Socrates and the showman, 20.
Spain, history of puppets in, 78-80.
Spectator, frequent mention of puppets, 151-152.
Stage, construction of (O'Neil), 226-229.
Statues, articulated, in Rome, 21. *See also* Idols; Images; Religious puppets.
Stentorella, Italian puppet character, 58.
Stevenson's *A Penny Plain and Twopence Colored*, quoted, 193-194.
Sthapaka, definition, 16.
Stoddard, Anne, describes production of *Three Wishes*, 186-187.
Sutradhara, definition, 16.
Symons, Arthur, on art of marionette, 206-207.

TATTERMANN, definition, 113.
Technique of production. *See* Producing a play.
Tempest, production described by Anatole France, 103-104.
Temptation of St. Anthony, by Rivière, 99-100.
Teoli, Italian marionettist, 61.
Teschner, Richard, marionette maker in Vienna, 133.
Thackeray's *Rose and the Ring* produced, 189-190, 200-201.
Théatines, order of monks, give spectacles, 83.
Théâtre des amis, history of, 92-94.

/ INDEX 241

Three Wishes, produced by Tony Sarg, 186-187.
Tintagiles. See *Death of Tintagiles*.
Titeres, Spanish puppets, 79.
Tocha, definition, 113.
Tokkenspiel, early subject matter, 114.
Tokyo, puppet plays in, 48.
Tombs, Egyptian, puppets found in, 16; jointed images found in Catacombs, 22.
Toone, Belgian showman, 140.
Torino, famous theatre in, 68-69; description of performance at Lupi theatre, 199-200.
Torriani, Giovanni, inventor, 78.
Toy theatres, 192-197.
Tragedy of Nauplius, representative Greek show, 19-20.
Travelling showmen, in Greece, 20; in Rome, 21; in China, 41; in Spain, 79; in Russia, 137-138; in London and rural England, 155.
Treat, Grace, 179.
Tschadar Chajal, puppet play of Turkestan, 30-31.
Turkestan, two types of puppets, 30.
Turkey, legends of origin of puppets, 36.
Types of puppets, on early Roman stage, 21; in Turkey, 37; in Italy, 54, 57-58.

VAN VOLKENBURG, Ellen, 174.
Variety bills follow Thirty Years' War in Germany, 123-125.

Vasari, quoted, on church spectacles, 51-52.
Venice, medieval puppets in, 67.
Vidusaka, Indian puppet buffoon, 34.
Vienna, the dolls of Richard Teschner, 133.
Voltaire's interest in puppets, 90.

WAR zone, French puppets in, 111-112.
Wayang dramas, Javanese shadow plays, 25-28.
Wheeler, Katherine, 174.
Wilkinsons, amateur English marionettists, 156-157.
Williamson, Mrs. Hamilton, 187-188.
Winter, Christoph, Cologne showman, 128.
Woltje, Belgian puppet buffoon, 140.
Writing for puppets, 217-218.
Wundt, Prof., on comic function of puppets, 203.
Wyspianski, Stanislaw, early plays with puppets, 196-197.

YEATS' *Shadowy Waters* produced in Cleveland, 182.
Yeddo, 18th century centre for puppet drama, 48.
Yorick (pseud.), on puppets in Egypt, 16; on growth of Greek puppetry, 18. See also Ferrigni.

ZELENKO, Alexander, quoted on modern Russian puppets, 137-138.

www.ingramcontent.com/pod-product-compliance
Lightning Source LLC
Chambersburg PA
CBHW031421150426
43191CB00006B/343